BEYOND BELIEF

ALSO BY RICHARD HOLLOWAY

Let God Arise
New Vision of Glory
A New Heaven

BEYOND BELIEF

The Christian Encounter with God

RICHARD HOLLOWAY

WILLIAM B. EERDMANS PUBLISHING COMPANY
GRAND RAPIDS, MICHIGAN

Library of Congress Cataloging in Publication Data

Holloway, Richard.
  Beyond belief.

    1. God. I. Title. II. Title: Christian encounter
with God.
BT102.H637   231   81-5438
ISBN 0-8028-3558-9   AACR2

FOR GRAHAM AND JANE

Contents

Acknowledgments

This book was written in the interstices of a rather busy life. Its composition was further complicated by the fact that I was transported to America from Scotland while it was being written. The fact that it is no worse than it actually is, is due to three people. My secretary, Martha Mitchell, typed the whole book, transforming a very scruffy manuscript into copy fit for the printer. I'm extremely grateful to her for that, and for much more. My wife, Jeannie, and my friend, Rusty Miller, corrected the proofs and made many valuable suggestions about improving the text. Between them, they tried to correct my rather headlong approach to punctuation. I'm very grateful to them.

The book is dedicated to Graham and Jane Forbes, who were beloved friends and colleagues at Old St. Paul's in Edinburgh for four years. I started the book at Old St. Paul's, and finished it at The Church of the Advent, Boston. I suppose, therefore, that it's a kind of *farewell* to one of these great congregations and a *hail* to the other.

All quotations are acknowledged in the text. I used the Revised Standard Version in quoting from the Bible.

The Church of the Advent   RICHARD HOLLOWAY
30 Brimmer Street   June 1981
Boston

PART ONE

The Adventure of Faith

CHAPTER ONE

Man in Search of God

You could say with considerable accuracy that we live in a
Peeping Tom society in the West today. We are all voyeurs.
We want stimulus without relationship. We want curiosity satisfied without commitment. As far as I understand the voyeur
or Peeping Tom in a narrowly sexual sense, he is usually someone who is afraid of or unable to sustain real contact with
another: he likes to keep the object of his need at a distance;
he doesn't want to get involved because involvement is arduous
and might bring failure. Is that not the characteristic mark of
our society as a whole? We are onlookers, spectators. As a matter of fact the average person in the West spends many hours
a week looking at television, which is the electronic perfection
of voyeurism. We spend a lot of time looking on. But television
is not the only phenomenon in our society which produces this
kind of distance between the watcher and the world. Tourism
does the same. Daniel Boorstin sees tourism as a kind of mobile
voyeurism. You speed through foreign cultures and societies
without really engaging with any of them: "It's Thursday, this
must be Rome." I daresay I'm exaggerating a bit, but I want
you to grasp one thing about our society which has important
effects upon religion. There is a new kind of mind around,
uninvolved, passive, unsurprised and deeply bored, purged of
expectation, impervious to mystery. The collective mind of our
society is lobotomized. And we are all affected by it. The spirit
of the age is deeply antipathetic toward the sense of the sacred,
which is the awareness that there exists a reality other than
ourselves which yet makes a claim upon us. It is important to

recognize this, because people who think they are believers have their beliefs profoundly modified by this prevailing attitude, and they are usually unaware of it. So there is a kind of formal and half-hearted belief around today which disfigures and distorts the Christian Faith—usually in the name of reason, but in fact because it suffers from a profound derangement of consciousness. That is an assertion which I shall try to substantiate later. Meanwhile let me return to my opening claim that we are all onlookers. I want us to stop and think and ask questions about the meaning of what we see.

Let us begin with a television program. It is a televised religious service, and it can be one you've actually watched. I have in mind the funeral service for Lord Mountbatten in Westminster Abbey. The place is packed with people, and we can, I think, rightly conclude that some of them at least are worshippers, believers. Prayers are addressed to an invisible presence. Hymns are sung, praising or imploring the same unseen reality. Scriptures are read and understood as, in some sense, the communication of that silent and unseen presence. Now, that complex activity we've just looked at can be explained away entirely in terms of what we can easily get at. There is nothing beyond it, so an explanation of it must be found on the purely human level. Explanations of this sort abound. But a question raises itself. At least some of the people present in that company believe that the explanation lies elsewhere. There is a hidden but real element to which the whole thing refers. Without that element the activity is meaningless. How can we gain knowledge of the unseen and silent partner to the mysterious conversation we call religious worship?

Now let us depart on a quick tour. Almost certainly we'll be led into one or two churches or cathedrals, and if we're wise we'll slip away from the tour guide and wander around on our own. In a dark and silent side-chapel we see a number of people kneeling. They are clearly not a gathering. They are individuals engaged in some silent but quite intense private activity. One old woman is fingering beads and muttering prayers under her breath. Again, the whole activity raises the question: Is there anyone else there? If you ask them what they're doing, they'll tell you they are praying, and praying, like worship, assumes the existence of that mysterious *something not ourselves* which is the other part of this activity. Without it the activity itself is irrational, though there may be a rational explanation for it. *Is* anybody there?

We'll go further, into strange cultures. If it's to the Middle East, we'll be surrounded by the pieces of the same puzzle. We'll find people engaged in public actions which in themselves are incomplete, irrational, and really rather silly. At certain points in the day they will unroll prayer mats, turn toward Mecca, and pray. If we visit Jerusalem we'll see, in that intensely secular city, many very old-fashioned-looking figures with strange locks of hair hanging down beneath large black hats. They are Hasidic Jews, a kind of charismatic sect within Judaism, so intense in their devotion to the unseen something that they pay scant regard to the ways of this century. They seem to live in an invisible atmosphere whose dominant reality is not accessible to us. Is anybody there, behind all this courageously unfashionable conduct?

Now let's try something much more difficult. Let's take a quick tour of the past. Here is a man called Paul of Tarsus writing to some friends; he is rather bitterly comparing himself to some teachers who have been disturbing his new converts.

> Are they servants of Christ? I am a better one—I am talking like a madman—with far greater labors, far more imprisonments, with countless beatings, and often near death. Five times I have received at the hands of the Jews the forty lashes less one. Three times I have been beaten with rods; once I was stoned. Three times I have been shipwrecked; a night and a day I have been adrift at sea; on frequent journeys, in danger from rivers, danger from robbers, danger from my own people, danger from Gentiles, danger in the city, danger in the wilderness, danger at sea, danger from false brethren; in toil and hardship, through many a sleepless night, in hunger and thirst, often without food, in cold and exposure. . . .

And why has he endured this awesome torturing and buffeting of what was by all accounts a frail body? In the service of his Lord Christ. Again, we see one side of something that makes no sense on its own. What we see is the effect of something else, some invisible cause, some prodigiously mysterious pressure that leads to conduct which by any standard is heroic beyond all description. Is Paul a madman, then? Is anybody there, and if so, how can he be known?

Let us come closer to our day, to the 16th century. All of us fear the mystery of death, and some will do anything to avoid it. Part of the anguish of untimely death is parting from those we love. Any father feels enormous pain at the thought of a death that would cut him off from his growing children— not to be there at their graduation, their marriage; not to be beside them when some of the shocks of life break upon them. We would do almost anything not to be robbed of that. Yet here is Thomas More, a family man who loved his children and longed to be with them to old age, locked up in the Tower of London: "Is not this house as nigh heaven as my own?" Mounting the scaffold: "I pray you, master Lieutenant, see me safe up, and my coming down let me shift for myself." Placing his head on the block he says to the executioner: "Pluck up thy spirits, man, and be not afraid to do thine office; my neck is very short; take heed therefore thou strike not awry, for saving of thine honesty." What is this kind of behavior about? Is the cool and affectionate Sir Thomas More in the grip of some irrational compulsion, or is there something beyond himself which gives him the rare power to defy death? Was there anybody beside him?

And here is the last stop on our tour. We have come back to our own century. It is April 9, 1945, at Flossenburg Concentration Camp in Germany. The camp doctor is writing:

> On the morning of that day between five and six o'clock the prisoners, among them Admiral Canaris, General Oster . . . and Reichsgerichtsrat Sack, were taken from their cells, and the verdicts of the court martial read out to them. Through the half-open door in one room of the huts I saw Pastor Bonhoeffer, before taking off his prison garb, kneeling on the floor praying fervently to his God. I was most deeply moved by the way this most lovable man prayed, so devout and so certain that God heard his prayer. At the place of execution, he again said a short

loves the outdoors.

To our scientific mailman.

E GIFT
E LOVES
TWELVE
YEAR:

onian

To Aunt Mary, the artistic one.

living thing.

uty in every

To Mom, who looks hopefully to the future.

To my best friend, the air and space fan.

To Dad, wh

To Tom, the history buff.

GIVE TH
EVERYON
TO OPEN
TIMES

Smiths

Sis, who loves to travel!

ompson, the bird watcher.

To Suzie, who se

prayer and then climbed the steps to the gallows, brave and composed. His death ensued after a few seconds. In the almost fifty years that I worked as a doctor, I have hardly ever seen a man die so entirely submissive to the will of God (quoted in Eberhard Bethge, *Dietrich Bonhoeffer*; London: Collins, 1977, p. 830).

The same baffling pattern, repeated again and again down the ages. Conduct which does not explain itself, which cannot account for itself without the presence of an elusive factor, some great power behind what we see that leads people to behave in ways that call forth a sort of anxious admiration.

Our tour is ended, but as we reflect on all that we've seen we are somewhat puzzled. The atheist in each of us is fascinated, irritated, and, finally, perhaps troubled by it. We seem to hear one part of an important conversation. No matter how closely we draw near to the speaker we can see, we cannot hear the other voice to which he listens so raptly. No matter how hard we look, we cannot see the light that seems to be reflected in his eyes. Now, some of that conduct has a kind of completeness even to us who see only one side of the encounter. Heroism, self-sacrifice has a kind of terrible beauty in it, a self-authenticating quality. But that is not the explanation offered by the people we are looking at, if they bother to offer us any. They claim that there is another actor at work, something we can't see or hear or make contact with, to which all their behavior refers. We see only an incomplete puzzle from which the crucial piece is missing. We hear only the baffling replies to a voice that is silent to us. We see only a reflected glory, a light that shines onto the faces of those we gaze upon, but we cannot find its source. There is behavior here that is inexplicable to us because some part of the equation is missing. We hear the sound of one hand clapping. Where is the other? We see lives that seem to respond to some great power beyond them, but we cannot find the place of its abiding. Is there something to which all this mysterious behavior refers? Is someone there all the time and we see him not? Or is the whole spectacle of religious behavior a moving but ultimately futile activity of projection of human need and longing upon the terrifyingly empty spaces of the cosmos? Are we orphaned and lonely children creating imaginary parents to console us for a loss that is absolute and unfillable? Is anybody there? Can we by searching find out God? Well, let's see.

Obviously, a search like this must be conducted, to a great extent, in our own heads. We know that God, if he exists, is not in space. Our search cannot be external, in space. It must be an inner search. Is God, then, in my head or discoverable by my head, my mind? Can the activity of my mind find God?

Before we embark upon this question let us try to answer another question. Does it matter whether we find out or not? God may or may not exist, so what? Life is too short to waste time on that issue. Well, the answer to that question is fairly simple. Life is not a straightforward thing that can be got on with. It brings with it all sorts of questions, and the most important question seems to be about life's very. meaning. We are born in some sense with the question because we are creatures who need meaning. There is an anxiety in us about life itself: how are we to live it? What are our values to be? What is it that awaits us? Is the universe indifferent to me? We may avoid these questions most of the time, but they hit us all sooner or later. As Robert Browning put it,

> Just when we are safest, there's a sunset touch,
> A fancy from a flower-bell, someone's death,
> A chorus-ending from Euripides. . . .

And up well the questions: what does it all mean? Has my life any purpose? No, the question of God is not just one question among many. It is the ground upon which all the others find or do not find their answers. I think the justification for this answer is found in the collapse of meaning and value in Western society. Western man is precisely the one who does not ask or answer the question, and as a consequence he is in a state of moral and personal confusion. Because he is now the creator of his own meaning, there is no one to whom he is responsible, so there is a massive flight from responsibility. Ours is the century, remember, in which more people have been killed in wars and purges than in any century before. Ours is the century not only of the discarding of whole peoples, but of the discarding of restraint and responsibility in relationships. Ours is

the throwaway century, the century in which all bonds dis-
solved, the century of the one-night-stand. Which of us has not
felt the pressure of all this upon us—the lifting of an external
restraint so that anything becomes possible? I'll return to this,
but for the moment let me repeat that the way we answer or
don't answer this question is momentous. Of course, we may
conclude that there is no God, that lostness and confusion is
to be our permanent condition, but surely it is worth taking
time to find out what the answer is because the question is so
momentous. The question of God or no God is the most important question there is, and only a diseased and trivialized
mind sees it as of no importance. If God there be, then it is of
the first importance that we find him since the meaning of our
life depends either upon him or upon ourselves, and we must
know which it is to be. There is no question greater than this.
Where do we look for answers?

Let's begin with some facts and some arguments, to see
how far they get us. Broadly speaking, there are three types of
arguments or "proofs" for the existence of God. The most basic
or foundational argument is really very simple, and it at least
begins with fact. It is possible to interpret the fact in various
ways, but it seems beyond dispute that when man is first found
in history, and wherever he is found, he has a mysterious sense
of being in the presence of, and in some way responsible to, a
power or powers beyond himself. Scholars of comparative religion call this the sense of the sacred, and it seems to be an
innate disposition. It is found not only at the beginning of
history but throughout history, up to but not necessarily including the present day. (I said earlier that modern Western
man seems to some extent to have had this sense cut out of
him.) Now, you can argue to various conclusions from the existence of this disposition in mankind, but one argument only
concerns me here. If this fact of the sense of the sacred or awe
or dread is *there*, what is the cause of which it is the effect? It
is an extraordinary state of mind or consciousness. Extraordinary in its universality and to a certain extent its unity and
coherence. The cause, the argument goes, must itself be extraordinary. The cause must be great enough to justify the
effect. The conviction of the existence of a transcendent reality
must be the result of the pressure of that reality upon the lives

of human beings. No other cause adequately fits the facts. You'll see, of course, that the argument begs the question. The thing is simply given. It is there in human nature, and there must be that to which it refers. Writing about this need in human nature, C. S. Lewis asks,

> Is there any reason to suppose that the universe offers any satisfaction to it? Nor does the being hungry prove that we have bread. But I think it may be urged that this misses the point. A man's physical hunger does not prove that man will get any bread; he may die of starvation on a raft in the Atlantic. But surely a man's hunger does prove that he comes of a race which repairs its body by eating and inhabits a world where eatable substances exist. In the same way, though I do not believe that my desire for Paradise proves that I shall enjoy it, I think it's a pretty good indication that such a place exists and that some men will. A man may love a woman and not win her; but it would be very odd if the phenomenon called 'falling in love' occurred in a sexless world (*The Weight of Glory*; London: S.P.C.K., 1954, p. 8).

Now, if you don't accept the common psychological explanation for the universal presence of the religious sense in man (which is, of course, that the whole thing is a self-generated and self-deluding activity of projection: "It would be nice if God existed. I like things to be nice. Therefore I shall decide that God exists." Incidentally, one of the most common fallacies about religion among unbelievers is that it's "nice" and "comforting" to believe in God. We'll see as we go further that that is far from the case), then it is perfectly logical to conclude that there must be something outside the natural realm that generates the need within man: it is either self-generated or it is generated from without.

I'll hurry over the next argument. It is sometimes called the Argument from Mind or Design. We are rational creatures endowed with minds which find patterns and designs in nature. Reason looks for and imposes pattern and meaning. We look for the meaning of things, the reason why things happen. Nature seems to be responsive to that tendency in us. But whence comes the pattern we claim to discern? If nature is in some sense responsive to our minds, is it not legitimate to argue that it is because nature itself is the result of Mind? We find meaning in it because it is the work of Mind. We do not impose pattern and law upon it. We discover the pattern, happen upon the Law. Whence came this? Some say, from Transcendent Mind or Reason.

The final argument looks within man. Man, it is claimed, is a moral creature. He feels himself to be under a mysterious sense of duty to follow the good and prefer it to the bad. (It does not matter for this argument that he can be deluded. What matters is that he finds some structure of moral preference within himself.) We find ourselves, then, owing duty to values outside ourselves, values which often conflict with our own apparent self-interest. We feel we ought to do certain things and ought to avoid others, and it is very difficult to give an entirely rational explanation of this. We just feel or believe that some things are right, others wrong. The philosopher Hume told us that you can't argue, anyway, from "is" to "ought." You must either abandon the sense of "oughtness" as irrational and unjustifiable or conclude that the mysterious demand you feel is imposed upon you by some source of value beyond yourself. You can conclude that the sense of duty has a cause in the existence of an attractive power of Goodness beyond yourself which exerts a magnetic influence upon you. It calls a recognition forth from you, the way beauty creates a response in you. We trust the sense we have that goodness is not just a matter of private taste or collective convenience but that it corresponds to what is Real. It imposes itself. Somehow, it authenticates itself. How can we account for this except by positing some transcendent source of value which communicates to our nature, plants the intuition in our hearts?

Related to this argument is another. We see that goodness is trampled upon and evil constantly triumphs, and this offends our sense of right and wrong. The wicked seem to go unpunished. This means that evil wins. Yet this offends our sense of justice and fitness. We conclude that if goodness and justice are to be vindicated, there has to be some transcendent reckoning, some judgment in which men will be shown the true order, the reality of things. How do we account for this indignation in us, this conviction that the true meaning of things is affronted and contradicted by the triumph of evil, if the universe is indifferent to value, unconcerned with goodness? If that is the case, whence comes this mysterious concern for righteousness? Why can't we just accept the existence of great evil and misery with the lack of concern shown in the animal kingdom? Whence comes this anger and resentment and conviction that something is out of tune? From the giver and creator of value; from God.

Now, these are ancient arguments and they probably don't convince many people today. The fact is, they have never convinced people. That has not been their function. They have served a different purpose. Men and women have *found* themselves convinced in some sense of the reality of God, prior to thinking about him. That's the way with most people. They are found believing. However, because we have minds there are always those who want their beliefs to be consistent with their reason, so they set about examining their beliefs, putting them in some sort of rational order. In other words, they reason *from* or *after* belief, not just *toward* belief. These arguments show at least this: that it is possible to give a rational account of belief, even if it is impossible to give a completely satisfactory set of reasons for believing. That said, what are we left with? Something, but not very much, I'm afraid. We have done our utmost, but it does not get us very far. How far has it taken us?

We may feel justified in concluding that there is no smoke without fire, but where is the fire? There are effects here, things we can see and hear, which seem to demand a cause, but we can't seem to find out much about it. What we have got is a hypothesis, a possibility, or, if we're very bold, a probability. There has to be something behind all this, we say; but what is that something, and what is it like? Well, let's play detective a little bit longer. Detectives build up a picture of a wanted man and end up with an approximate likeness; an "identikit," they call it. Let's see if we can do that with God. Before we begin we have to recognize one difficulty. When the detective builds up a picture of a wanted man, he produces a pictorial approximation, he does not produce the man. He produces a clumsy and faulty but useful impression of the man. When we build up a picture of God we're even further from the reality than that. The wanted man is at least a man, so our attempt to describe him will not be totally in the dark. We won't give him two heads and tractor wheels instead of feet. That's not so with God. So far we've no idea what God is like, and in order to build up a picture we have to use human categories. What we end up with is a very, very remote approximation, but it's all we can do. We say, very well, we know there must be a colossal distance between God and us, nevertheless we've got to come up with something, so let's build up what we can on the basis of our own human experience. Let's try to draw a human likeness, however inadequate, and it'll be something.

With that major modification in mind, what have men and women come up with in their identikit picture of God? Briefly and broadly speaking, they have projected onto God three characteristics or marks or attributes: Personality, Rationality, and Morality. The basis for this projection is simple: these are the three outstanding characteristics of man, and God, by definition, must be at least as high as the highest we know. God cannot be an impersonal force, like electricity, because you cannot relate to a force; you can only relate to a person. In the same way, then, there must be Personality in God. And God can't be arbitrary and capricious in his nature, like a spoiled child or an immature Roman emperor. There must be purpose and reason and meaning in his nature because they are the highest attributes of mature adults. And God must have a concern for value. Our own dim appreciation of goodness and righteousness must find some reflection or echo in his nature. Personality. Rationality. Morality. There's our identikit picture, then. We have produced a hypothesis, a supposition, to fill the great Question Mark; and we've sketched onto it three features, but we certainly have not produced God or much to warm the heart. By a process of inference we have put together a kind of picture of an absent and elusive reality.

Say you stumbled upon an unlocked cabin in the woods. It is empty, but there are things around that indicate it is lived in. By examining them you can put together some sort of idea of the person who lives there, but just because you have the idea, even the conviction, that someone owns the cabin, you cannot be said to know him or have a relationship with him. He's just a hypothesis, unless he walks in the door as you stand looking around at his possessions. If he doesn't, you are left wondering, perhaps even longing. That's the way it is between us and God, so far. If he stubbornly refuses to walk in the door, is there anything else we can do? Yes, there is something else, and it brings us to the next stage of our investigation.

Our minds have taken us as far as the shaky conviction that the elusive person exists. There is an owner of the cabin, and since he still does not present himself to us we have to continue our investigation as best we can. One way is to listen to people who claim to know him, who claim to be in touch with him. We call such people witnesses, and what they say we can think of as their testimony. In any religious search you have to spend a lot of time both assessing the integrity of the witnesses and weighing their testimony. We have minds, and we must not leave them aside in this activity because the area of religion is filled with deluded as well as healthy witnesses; it is filled with false testimony as well as true. History is filled with false messiahs; it is littered with corrupt religions. We dare not leave our reason out of all this, although we won't expect our reason alone to get us all the way. Well then, there are witnesses for God, people who claim to know him, who claim to speak on his behalf. "Thus says the Lord," they say; not "I think" or "It is my opinion that . . . ," but "Thus says the Lord."

Is it reasonable, in principle, to think that this can happen, that God can so communicate to and through others? It may not have happened to me, but that's true of a lot of things. I have not heard the music that forced its way into the consciousness of Mozart or Beethoven or Bach, but I have to believe they did. I have not heard the poetry that forced its way into the consciousness of William Shakespeare or T. S. Eliot, but I have to believe they did. I can see no reason, in principle, why God, if he exists, cannot invade the consciousness, the dreams, cannot indeed conquer the very resistance of men and women by the direct inspiration of his presence. Indeed, having thought about it, I'd be surprised if he didn't. So I do not find the idea impossible that God can and does choose special witnesses as the channels of his revelation of himself. And we've just come to an important word, Revelation. We have seen, and it should not surprise us, that we have not been able by our searching and action to find God, to uncover his nature. Nor can we with persons. They have to disclose themselves, open themselves to us, reveal their hearts by a voluntary act of self-disclosure. Revelation, God's disclosure of himself, is the key category in religion, and we don't—many of us—like it much. It disarms our pride, our confidence in our ability to master all things, even the things of God. We like to be in control, and revelation reverses all that. It calls for silence and obedience and acceptance when we want to interrogate, object, and assert. Revelation cuts through all our diversionary chatter and silences us.

> You are not here to verify,
> Instruct yourself, or inform curiosity
> Or carry report. You are here to kneel. . . .

Who, then, are these witnesses through whom we receive knowledge of God at a secondary level? There have been many and of various quality. No age, no society has been without them, but the most impressive and conclusive have been the Jewish prophets. Here we come up against another key category in religion, Election. It seems to be undeniable that certain persons are "elected" by God to a special role in his activity of self-disclosure. This strategy of divine election seems to have been concentrated with particular intensity upon one people, the Jews. To them was given the central role in that process of education whereby God prepared men and women to receive knowledge of himself. And you don't have to accept this on anyone's word. Study the facts, read the record, open yourself to the testimony they left. Of course there is a lot of dross mixed in with the gold of inspiration, but the overall effect is overwhelming and compelling, if you can but bring some freshness to it, if you can but lay aside your jaded scepticism and hear what they say. When you open yourself to it, it brings with it a heartbreaking sense of that mystery we long to fathom; it seems to be brushed with the fire of God's own burning love and anguish. The God who is disclosed is a heartbroken God, a God of burning holiness and purity who longs to draw us more and more into his own likeness, who sends forth prophets and teachers to call us back, to appeal to us to turn around, to seek the reality of his love. He is a God consumed with a holy ambition for us, longing, pleading for our peace—and we would not. He is like a faithful and tender husband who forgives our adulteries time and again, wooing us to return to him. He is a god baffled and wounded by our perversity, our self-loathing, our cruelty to ourselves and each other, our trampling upon the weak, our unrighteousness. He is a god who is stung into judgment and rebuke. Oh, this god is no comfort to us at all, or not in the short run. He is no comforting projection of our needs. And those to whom he comes and who come to us in his name have no enviable vocation, they are not high on a spiritual narcotic: they are "despised, despised and rejected." God is no fleecy blanket to wrap around us and protect us from the chill of cosmic loneliness. He is a disturber of our complacence. He is a lion roaring in the woods, a fire blazing, a sword smiting. We may have conducted our leisurely and evasive search for God, but, say the prophets, we don't really want to find or be found by him, because he would burn us up. "Our God is a consuming fire," not a hot-water bottle. Because we have desecrated his world! We are his children and he is our Father, and we have rebelled against him and gone into the far country away from him.

> Hear, O heavens, and give ear, O earth; for the Lord has spoken: "Sons have I reared and brought up, but they have rebelled against me. The ox knows its owner, and the ass its master's crib; but Israel does not know, my people does not understand" (Isaiah 1:2f.).

So he raises up witnesses, voices crying in the wilderness to call us, call us back. And we stone the prophets and kill those he sends after us. We stop our ears. We don't want to hear that burning and pleading voice. Because, were we to hear it, it would break us down, and which of us wants that—to own our need, to cry like lost children, to throw ourselves upon the fire of his love? We don't want it now, nor did they want it then. The history of prophecy in Israel is the story of a magnificent defeat. But let us listen to some of its sounds.

> When Israel was a child, I loved him, and out of Egypt I called my son. The more I called them, the more they went from me. . . . Yet it was I who taught Ephraim to

walk, I took them up in my arms; but they did not know that I healed them. I led them with cords of compassion, with the bands of love. . . . (Hosea 11:1ff.).

Let me sing for my beloved a love song concerning his vineyard: My beloved had a vineyard on a very fertile hill. He digged it and cleared it of stones, and planted it with choice vines; he built a watchtower in the midst of it, and hewed out a wine vat in it; and he looked for it to yield grapes, but it yielded wild grapes. And now, O inhabitants of Jerusalem and men of Judah, judge, I pray you, between me and my vineyard. What more was there to do for my vineyard, that I have not done in it? When I looked for it to yield grapes, why did it yield wild grapes? And now I will tell you what I will do to my vineyard. I will remove its hedge, and it shall be devoured; I will break down its wall, and it shall be trampled down. I will make it a waste; it shall not be pruned or hoed and briers and thorns shall grow up; I will also command the clouds that they rain no rain upon it. For the vineyard of the Lord of hosts is the house of Israel, and the men of Judah are his pleasant planting; and he looked for justice, but behold, bloodshed; for righteousness, but behold, a cry! (Isaiah 5:1-7).

"Come to Bethel, and transgress; to Gilgal, and multiply transgression; bring your sacrifices every morning, your tithes every three days: Offer a sacrifice of thanksgiving of that which is leavened, and proclaim freewill offerings, publish them; for so you love to do, O people of Israel!" says the Lord God. "I gave you cleanness of teeth in all your cities, and lack of bread in all your places, yet you did not return to me," says the Lord. "And I also withheld the rain from you when there were yet three months to the harvest; I would send rain upon one city, and send no rain upon another city; one field would be rained upon, and the field on which it did not rain withered" (Amos 4:4-7).

"Go, and proclaim these words toward the north, and say, 'Return, faithless Israel, says the Lord. I will not look on

you in anger, for I am merciful, says the Lord; I will not
be angry for ever' " (Jeremiah 3:12).

"Is Ephraim my dear son? Is he my darling child? For as
often as I speak against him, I do remember him still.
Therefore my heart yearns for him; I will surely have
mercy on him, says the Lord" (Jeremiah 31:20).

The prophets put you in touch with a terrible wrestling within
the divine love: God's purpose for us, his ambition for us,
wrestles with his compassion. He knows whereof we are made,
he remembers that we are but dust; but he longs to draw us
into his glory; he offers us a share in the divine nature. You
can feel the passionate exasperation of God as he coaxes, ca-
joles, entices us; and then is stung into blazing anger by our
slowness, our ignorance of the things belonging to our peace.
The God of the prophets is a passionate, grieving God, a God
who acts, who calls to us through history and tragedy and the
best of our own heart.

On the night Blaise Pascal experienced the burning reality of God's presence he wrote these words on a scrap of paper
which he ever afterward kept close to his heart:

> From about half past ten in the evening to
> about half an hour after midnight.
>   Fire.
> God of Abraham, God of Isaac, God of Jacob,
> Not the God of philosophers and scholars.

Not the God of the philosophers. Not an abstraction, a
hypothesis, a theory which does nothing except provide subject
matter for doctoral dissertations, but the living, burning God
who showed himself to the prophets and who would show
himself to us; the real God who spoke to men we can name,
like Abraham and Isaac and Jacob and Amos and Hosea and
Isaiah and Jeremiah. The God we seek after is a vivid and
alarmingly personal God. As we draw near to the end of the
story of prophetic failure we sense the anguish and bafflement
of God, whose overtures were spurned. He was in the world
but the world received him not. He came unto his own people,

chosen to bring his truth to the nations, and his own people received him not. The wayfaring God is kept out of men's lives, always pushed away to the periphery, never gaining an entry. So the Old Testament ends on a note of baffled longing and bewildered hope, expressed in the poetry of inspired desire.

"The Lord whom you seek will suddenly come to his temple; the messenger of the covenant in whom you delight, behold, he is coming, says the Lord of hosts. But who can endure the day of his coming, and who can stand when he appears?" (Malachi 3:1-2).

CHAPTER TWO

God in Search of Man

"**C**anst thou by searching find out God? Canst thou find out the Almighty unto perfection? It'is high as heaven; what canst thou do? Deeper than the grave; what canst thou know?" That quotation from Job (11:7f.) provides us with a suitable opening for recalling what we said in the first chapter. Job was right: we cannot by searching find out God. It is true that the action of our minds as it searches for meaning in reality may be led to a persuasive hypothesis: there must be Something Not Ourselves behind all that is. We may even attribute to that insubstantial idea some characteristics which we feel it must logically have. But we are left with something cold and speculative. We cannot in any sense be said to "know" what we have postulated. In a very real sense, too, it remains the creature of our minds. It is a projection of our own reasoning. It is our idea. We may say that there has to be something which can adequately account for the idea. But even if we accept that claim as having some power, we are still left with very little. It is certain that we cannot by searching find out God. However, these remarks presuppose that we are the only active agents in this enterprise. It is a human activity. It was here that we made our first jump. There is certainly no logical reason to suppose that the reality we are searching for is not also active, is not also searching. If we are at all near the mark we would expect the elusive mystery we long to know to make himself known. This is precisely the claim that is made. The main category in religion is Revelation, the self-disclosure of God. There is a whole range of experience known to some of the most fascinating and noble human beings ever born, which they describe as the inspiration of God, the pressure of that great mystery upon their hearts and minds. It enters their lives with disturbing and unavoidable power so that they feel themselves to be the very organ by which God addresses man. "Thus says the Lord" is their baffling but accustomed form of address. And we find this burning certainty at its noblest and most illuminating in the lives of the Hebrew prophets, who were given words that still stab the heart and disturb the mind and challenge the feebleness and cowardice of our lives. What are the main characteristics of the prophetic message? Let me offer an analogy.

One of the important if fashionable sciences of our day is ecology. The word comes from the Greek word for house, and other familiar words such as economics and ecumenics are derived from it. The *Oxford English Dictionary* defines ecology as "The branch of biology which deals with the mutual relations between organisms and their environment," and then goes on to provide a second definition, "their mutual relations collectively." The word has been given a much wider meaning in contemporary debate, but basic to its sense is that balance or harmony which characterizes the natural order when it is left to fulfill its own law. When this balance is interrupted by, for instance, the extermination of a species, the whole harmony is destroyed and the effects are felt throughout the system. One of the great accusations made against the people of the postindustrial world is that they have arrogantly and crudely violated the sensitive balance of nature by their greed, with consequences with which we are all familiar. This idea that catastrophe awaits those who overstep natural limits has, in fact, been around for a long time. The Greeks called this particular kind of arrogance "hubris" and its consequence "nemesis."

I don't think it is fanciful to see a specific application of this phenomenon at the heart of the prophetic message. The prophets warn us against the consequences of a certain kind of conduct. There is, they say, a moral or spiritual ecology in the universe, a divinely imposed harmony, which requires an appropriate response from mankind. The code word for this spiritual ecology is Covenant. There are two covenants in the Old Testament. The first can be described as an implicit covenant; it is the covenant of creation. By his creation man is in a covenant relationship with God. This relationship does not work by a process of automatic natural balance as in subhuman creation, but by willed cooperation and consent. The best model is the family, which is the original economy and requires restraint and sensitivity to the rights and dignity of others if it is to achieve harmony. The model of behavior which is offered to man is that of God himself, who went forth from himself in an act of expressive love in creation and who calls for a like response from man. Man is to go *out* toward his neighbor and toward God. Man is woven into a complex fabric of relationships, but they don't work automatically. Fatefully, God has given man freedom so that his response will be a voluntary, willed agreement with God. In a real sense man is a co-creator with God in the bringing into existence of a spiritual order. This freedom is fateful, because noncooperation is possible. One of the keen points of the prophetic message is that man has, in fact, broken the covenant of creation. The opposite tendency to that going-out from the self which is the characteristic of the divine nature is absorption in the self, narcissism. We become our own world, our own God, and everything in all creation is made to take a secondary role; everything outside the self becomes a bit part in the endless little television serial of our life. Nothing *is* except in relation to Me. So from the beginning the pattern, the balance, the covenant-ecology is distorted.

There are two dramatic consequences. First of all, there is a profound distortion of our sense of God. Since we are the only thing that is really real to ourselves, God's reality becomes vague and unimpressive. Our awareness of prevailing mystery becomes blunted and weak. We end up autistic creatures, certain only of our own existence. And a further development follows from this. When we sense God at all, we seek to manipulate him. Since we are real and everything else is vague, we make God in our own image, the better to use him. Magic is one manifestation of this, but certain kinds of superpatriotism can be another. Magical religions buy God off. We know that every man has his price. Why not every God? So religion becomes an elaborate appeasement process, crude or refined according to your sensibilities. This is one of the roots of sacrifice; significantly, sacrifice was one of the targets of the prophetic wrath.

> "I hate, I despise your feasts, and I take no delight in your solemn assemblies. Even though you offer me your burnt offerings and cereal offerings, I will not accept them, and the peace offerings of your fatted beasts I will not look upon. Take away from me the noise of your songs; to the melody of your harps I will not listen. But let justice roll down like waters, and righteousness like an ever-flowing stream" (Amos 5:21ff.).

Of course there is a germ of truth in the practice of sacrifice. Behind it was a recognition that the only appropriate response to God is self-offering. But even this absolutely proper intuition has been corrupted, and sacrifice became a vast manipulative exercise which by the time of Jesus offered innumerable opportunities for the temple authorities in Jerusalem to make money. God became a kind of super-celestial consumer who was bought off by impressive bribes. And don't think that religion has moved on very much. Manipulation of the divine is a permanent human characteristic, more dangerous, indeed, in its more subtle and refined forms.

The second consequence of the breaking of the covenant balance is its effect on human beings, although here it is difficult to separate cause from effect. If the first consequence was the objectification of God into an idol to be appeased and manipulated, the second consequence is the objectification of the neighbor. My neighbor becomes not Thou but You or It. My brothers and sisters cease to be centers of intrinsic significance, persons. They become, as God became, a bit vague, not really there. I am the central character and they revolve around me. I am the Prince of Denmark, and they are only there as foils to my central role. We'll come back to this phenomenon again and again, but it is important to recognize that it is the truth about ourselves. We are mysteriously guilty of an original narcissism or autism which enshrines the self as judge of reality and value and significance. Of course, it makes us all miserable because the self cannot be enjoyed in that way. We cannot devour ourselves and be healthily nourished. It is this radical and primary choosing of the self which lies at the root of all misery and every great tragedy in history. All the great disaster scenarios in the Old Testament are related to this theme of the nemesis we bring on ourselves when we arrogantly distort the proper balance of reality. The Flood and the Destruction of the Cities of the Plain are both the consequences of human inflation. Man tears a great rent in the fabric of the natural and spiritual order by his sin. "Ah, sinful nation, a people laden with iniquity, offspring of evildoers, sons who deal corruptly! They have forsaken the Lord, they have despised the Holy One of Israel, they are utterly estranged." Estranged? Made strangers! Lost in a cosmic and personal wilderness.

This is the world situation with which God has to deal. It is presupposed by the prophets and to a great extent influenced the writing in the Old Testament even of the non-prophetic books. What we have there is history as seen from God's position. It is very important to recognize the distinctive mark of the biblical-prophetic understanding of God. There are various forms of theism, but they can be loosely subdivided into three. Without imposing too technical a meaning upon it, we can call the first form "Deism." The God of the deist is remote and detached from his creation. He set it going and it bears his imprint upon it. Just as a clever antique dealer looks for the hallmark which will help him date and evaluate an old piece of silver, so the wise man learns to discover the clues which God has stamped upon his creation. In both cases, however, the original author is no longer on the scene. His activity was concentrated upon the act of creation. Since then he has left it to its own devices.

At the other extreme are a group of views which can be loosely described as pantheistic. Pantheism appears to make no distinction between God and creation at all. It comes in crude forms, but it can also be more subtle. What it seems to do is to rule out any possibility of divine autonomy or freedom to act in a way that appears contrary to the plan of nature. God is not able to take extraordinary steps. He is not able to act with unpredictable initiative. In some real sense he is tied in to a rigid system.

A moment's reflection will make you see that both of these views have something in common: their model of God tends to be mechanistic or impersonal, and it leaves no room for the freedom to act, to make a difference. The freedom to take initiatives is the very genius of personality. It is important to grasp this because behind many of the claims which are made on behalf of different critical schools of theology is often a set of unexpressed assumptions about God. Your idea of God will color your attitude to the claim that is made by the New Testament, for instance. We may think we are approaching the evidence with open minds. In fact our governing ideas profoundly affect our approach to events, and for that reason we ought to know what our governing ideas are.

The prophets' governing idea was the freedom and transcendence of God. There is nothing speculative or abstract in the prophetic teaching about God. The central idea the prophets wished to express was the sovereign freedom of God to *act*, to accomplish his purposes. An abstract idea of God as "the uncaused cause" behind the system of the universe or a speculative idea of God as inhering in and being limited by "the things that are seen" would have seemed madness to them. God was the Creator of the universe who inhabited eternity yet who stooped down to involve himself in the destiny of the children he had created. The two technical words which are used to describe this paradox are Transcendence and Immanence, but they are as misleading as they are inevitable. What they seek to assert is that God is apart from his creation and prior to it: before the creation God *was*. Nevertheless, God is intimately involved in his creation. "The heavens are telling the glory of God; and the firmament proclaims his handiwork." The category of the personal is the best way of capturing both modes of God's activity. After all, we know that a person is an independent identity who, nevertheless, can be intimately involved in our lives. I repeat, it is the primacy of the personal which is the main burden of the message of the prophets. We must not think of God as Force, or Law, or Principle, or Cause, or Order, or anything other than Person. Perhaps the best way to capture the fact that the two modes of God's activity are essentially the working of his sovereign freedom is to quote a marvelous verse from Isaiah.

Thus says the high and lofty One who inhabits eternity, whose name is Holy: "I dwell in the high and holy place, and also with him who is of a contrite and humble spirit" (57:15).

Now, it is a fact that men and women shrink from the prophetic teaching about God. If they are clever they will say it is naive or anthropomorphic. The reason, however, lies deeper. You see, we can cope with other ideas of God because they keep him at a distance; he never gets too close. He's either so remote as not to exist for any practical purpose, or we encounter him at a second or third remove in a way that insulates his burning reality from us. That suits us absolutely! It means that God does not complicate or get involved in our lives except in such a vague way as really to leave us in charge. We don't really want what Eliot called "the ruined millionaire" erupting untidily on to the scene we have learned how to control. Most of us are practical atheists. We have to be, because the alternative is a type of surrender that makes us wince with foreboding. Our God is a consuming fire, but rather than draw near and be consumed we prefer to play academic games with him. Clever people, as I've said, are very good at this. They can always find reasons for delay, for putting off the moment of final surrender. Nowhere is this described with greater insight and tactfulness than in the prayer Evelyn Waugh puts into the mouth of St. Helena, mother of the Emperor Constantine. It is addressed to the three Wise Men who were led to Jesus.

> Like me, you were late in coming. The shepherds were here long before; even the cattle. They had joined the chorus of angels before you were on your way. How laboriously you came, taking sights and calculating where the shepherds had run barefoot! How odd you looked on the road, attended by what outlandish liveries, laden with such preposterous gifts!
> You came at length to the final stage of your pilgrimage and the great star stood still above you. What did you do? You stopped to call on King Herod. Deadly exchange of compliments in which there began that un-

ended war of mobs and magistrates against the innocent!

Yet you came and were not turned away. You too found room before the manger. Your gifts were not needed, but they were accepted and put carefully by, for they were brought with love. In that new order of charity that had just come to life, there was room for you too. You were not lower in the eyes of the holy family than the ox or the ass.

You are my especial patrons, and patrons of all latecomers, of all who have a tedious journey to make to the truth, of all who are confused with knowledge and speculation, of all who through politeness make themselves partners in guilt, of all who stand in danger by reason of their talents.

Dear Cousins, pray for me, and for my poor overloaded son. May he, too, before the end find kneeling-space in the straw. Pray for the great, lest they perish utterly. . . .

For his sake who did not reject your curious gifts, pray always for all the learned, the oblique, the delicate. Let them not be quite forgotten at the Throne of God when the simple come into their kingdom (*Helena*; London: Chapman and Hall, 1950, p. 239).

You see, for all of us, clever or simple, God must become Thou, must become Person. When he has become that, we'll expect and not be surprised by actions which are *personal*. Think about your own lives. Most of us lead lives of an even and predictable tenor. However, the real genius of our nature is that, when circumstances demand, we can take sudden and unpredictable action to deal with the emergency. We impose our personality upon events, we do not allow events to control our personality. We rise up and act; and so does God. He does not lie there in remote ineffectiveness, either disinterested or content to delegate his responsibility to impersonal intermediaries. This God of ours is a God who acts, who gets involved, who meets people. His activity seems to be on two levels. First of all, there is the level of "the collective-historical." This is partly an outworking of the moral dynamic of the universe. "God is not mocked." Man cannot forever run against the grain of moral reality and get away with it. So God's action is seen remotely in the great judgments of history.

But an equally important level of divine action is "the personal-vocational." In order to save many God concentrates on a few. He makes his appeal known to all through some. He sends forth his word into the hearts and minds of his chosen witnesses, who are burdened with the mystery of the divine word within them.

Before moving on to explore this activity of God, let me repeat, at the risk of tediousness, the central claim the prophets make. The personal, not the impersonal, is the primary category of the biblical knowledge of God. Persons rouse themselves; they take extraordinary steps to guard their interests and protect those they love. They go to inordinate and unpredicatable lengths for those they love. So does God.

At last we have arrived at the other covenant in the Old Testament, the covenant proper. If the covenant of creation can be thought of in some sense as impersonal, the second is clearly and defiantly personal and particular, at least at its inception. It is the covenant of Special Election, the choosing of Israel as a special intermediary, a light to lighten the Gentiles. The very word "covenant" underlines the personalist characteristic of the event. A covenant is a relationship between two persons or groups. The Prayer Book talks of marriage as "the vow and covenant betwixt them made." A covenant is a bonding, a pledging. "I will be your God, and you will be my people." This is the Old Covenant or Testament. I have described it as personal and vocational at its inception, but that was not always to be its main note. The curse of all religion is formalism, external conformity to the letter of a covenant rather than internal acceptance of its spirit. The Old Covenant was cursed from the start by formalism. In the first place it was to some extent a collective contract between God and a people, written on tables of stone, the tables of the covenant, the Ten Commandments. Secondly, like many marriages, only one of the partners entered it with full intention and commitment. Because of the fact of its external expression in the Ten Commandments it was prone to the wrong sort of conformism. It was never wholehearted on the side of Israel, and while the internal commitment waned the external form waxed into a vast proliferation of rules and regulations, six hundred and thirteen of them by the time of Jesus. What happened was that the human tendency at all times to depersonalize relationships and substitute manipulation and exploitation and institutionalism asserted itself. You see it all the time. People become *clients* to social workers, *patients* to doctors, *voters* to politicians, *customers* to shopkeepers, and *statistics* to clergymen; we all become *numbers* to innumerable institutions. The sacred nature of the personal is abandoned and the other becomes, in some profound sense, a thing to be manipulated, feared, enjoyed, exploited. And we do it with God. He ceases to be Thou and becomes It. *We* forsake the covenant, and so did Israel, not necessarily according to the letter but increasingly according to the spirit. So this covenant, too, is forsaken, and God continues to long after his children and to grieve for them and burn with anger at them. All this is expressed by the prophets. We hear in them the very heartbeat of God's love and wrath.

And the longing grows for a new covenant, not this time mediated by men and inscribed on tables of stone, but mediated by God himself and inscribed on the very hearts of his children.

> "Behold, the days are coming, says the Lord, when I will make a new covenant with the house of Israel and the house of Judah, not like the covenant which I made with their fathers when I took them by the hand to bring them out of the land of Egypt, my covenant which they broke, though I was their husband, says the Lord. But this is the covenant which I will make with the house of Israel after those days, says the Lord: I will put my law within them, and I will write it upon their hearts; and I will be their God, and they shall be my people. And no longer shall each man teach his neighbor and each his brother, saying, 'Know the Lord,' for they shall all know me, from the least of them to the greatest, says the Lord; for I will forgive their iniquity, and I will remember their sin no more" (Jeremiah 31:31ff.).

This longing wells up in the Old Testament and focusses on the expectation of the Messiah, the Lord's Anointed, who would be the mediator of a better, more effective covenant. Even this deep longing became corrupted into a political instrument, however, whereby the Coming One was seen as a vindicator of Israel before the world, an ecclesio-political leader, who would fulfil Israel's latent desire to be a power among the powers of the world. In the Old Testament itself, however, are embedded a series of baffling and eloquent prophecies which point in a completely different direction. They sing in beautiful poetry of one who would rescue and redeem, not by an act of *power* but by suffering and rejection. These prophecies were to provide a potent source of meditation and interpretation by the Christian movement, but they were never really interpreted messianically by Israel. Nevertheless, there they lay in the Old Testament, bafflingly alien to the dominant hope, like a meteor from another planet lying in the basement of a tower-block in Babylon till its time might come.

> Who has believed what we have heard? And to whom has the arm of the Lord been revealed? For he grew up before him like a young plant, and like a root out of dry ground; he had no form or comeliness that we should look at him, and no beauty that we should desire him. He was despised and rejected by men; a man of sorrows, and acquainted with grief; and as one from whom men hide their faces he was despised, and we esteemed him not.
>
> Surely he has borne our griefs and carried our sorrows; yet we esteemed him stricken, smitten by God, and afflicted. But he was wounded for our transgressions, he was bruised for our iniquities; upon him was the chastisement that made us whole, and with his stripes we are healed. All we like sheep have gone astray; we have turned every one to his own way; and the Lord has laid on him the iniquity of us all. He was oppressed, and he was afflicted, yet he opened not his mouth; like a lamb that is led to the slaughter, and like a sheep that before its shearers is dumb, so he opened not his mouth. . . .
>
> Yet it was the will of the Lord to bruise him; he has put him to grief; when he makes himself an offering for sin, he shall see his offspring, he shall prolong his days;

the will of the Lord shall prosper in his hand; he shall
see the fruit of the travail of his soul and be satisfied; by
his knowledge shall the righteous one, my servant, make
many to be accounted righteous; and he shall bear their
iniquities (Isaiah 53).

The final effect of the Old Testament upon us is a sense
of magnificent incompleteness, though I have given it but scant
attention. In a few breathless pages I have tried to suggest
something of the drama of the religious formation of the Jewish people. What I have entirely failed to suggest is something
of the slowness of this process of education by God of his people through the prophets and the crises of their history. Most
of us have a very compressed view of history, anyway. We fail
to note how slow is our own spiritual formation and how uncertain. From Moses to Christ is a period of thirteen hundred
years. If we recall how slowly the political constitution of England evolved from the Norman Conquest in 1066 to the present day, we'll have some sort of measure for the distance we're
having to cover. And Israel only existed as a kingdom for a
very short time. David became king in 1016 BC, and for the
next five hundred years Israel struggled against the hostile
empires that surrounded her. The main period of prophetic
activity in Israel was from the 8th century to the 5th century
before Christ. It was during this time that the ideas we have
been discussing were impressed upon the tradition of Jewish
religion. From the 8th century to the 2nd century the Old
Testament as we know it was coming to be. In 586 BC Jerusalem
fell and the temple was destroyed. Israel never really existed
as an autonomous state again. This was the beginning of that
dispersion of the Jews throughout the world which has been
their unique characteristic, apart from the tenacity of their
faith. It is true that their land was resettled and the Temple
rebuilt under the Persian Empire, but by that time the planting
of the prophetic doctrine of God in most of the centers of the
civilized world had occurred. By the same mysterious economy,
the period that saw the beginning of the spread of the prophetic word also witnessed the end of living prophecy. "We do
not see our signs; there is no longer any prophet, and there
is none among us who knows how long," cried the Psalmist

(74:9). Meditation upon the prophetic tradition continued, of course, but it no longer had that freshness and newness that characterized the prophets. The writings that came after, including Proverbs and Job, attained a high level of wisdom (it is called "Wisdom literature"), but it often lacks that revelatory quality which marks the prophets.

It is difficult to avoid science-fiction imagery to describe what had happened. An intense period of spiritual activity concentrated upon a particular people, who are then blown to the four corners of the earth while the seeds sown germinate and spread and do their work. And the world, too, can be seen as being prepared for what was to come. There was in the ancient world a tremendous sense of both failure and longing. The great empires of the East, Babylonia and Persia, with their luxury and cruelty, demonstrated that an opulent paganism may for a time stir the blood but that it always fails to satisfy the heart. Yet it had been these empires which had provided the agents and the theater of the Jewish dispersion. They were spiritually infertile themselves, but they were carriers of the divine seed. In contrast to the cruel empires of the East, we have always looked back with admiration upon the Greek Empire and its civilizing mission. But nostalgia can blind us to the failure of the Greek spirit, its sense of its own incompleteness, summed up in the wistful words Plato put into the mouth of Simmias in the *Phaedo*, where the question of the immortality of the soul is under discussion.

> It seems to me, Socrates, as to you also, I fancy, that it is very difficult, if not impossible, in this present life to have clear knowledge concerning such subjects; but that, on the other hand, it is the mark of a faint-hearted spirit to desist from examining all that is said about them in every way, or to abandon the search so long as there is any chance of light anywhere. For on such subjects one ought to secure one of two things, either to learn or discover the truth, or, if this is impossible, at least to get the best of the human argument [words] and hardest to refute, and relying on this as on a raft, to sail the perilous sea of life, unless one were able, more securely and less peril-

ously, to make one's journey upon a safer vessel upon some divine word (*Pheado* 85 C–D).

Yet Greek civilization provided an important unifying element: its language. Greek was the lingua franca of the ancient world, and it was in this language that the new universal religion was to find its fittest expression.

Finally, there was the great Roman power; and there is plenty of evidence of the cynicism and longing that existed in the best minds of its sons. It showed that human power and the will to dominate are not sufficient to save and satisfy mankind; yet Rome also furnished the highways along which the new message was to spread, and it provided the order and control that allowed it to spread so rapidly.

Empires rose and fell and left their complicated effect upon world history and upon Israel. And Israel, or some in Israel, waited and watched, looking for the consolation of Israel. The visions had faded, there was not one prophet more, inspiration had failed. And then,

> In the fifteenth year of the reign of Tiberius Caesar, Pontius Pilate being governor of Judea, and Herod being tetrarch of Galilee, and his brother Philip tetrarch of the region of Ituraea and Trachonitis, and Lysanias tetrarch of Abilene, in the high-priesthood of Annas and Caiaphas, the word of God came to John the son of Zechariah in the wilderness; and he went into all the region about the Jordan, preaching a baptism of repentance for the forgiveness of sins. As it is written in the book of the words of Isaiah the prophet, "The voice of one crying in the wilderness: Prepare the way of the Lord, make his paths straight. Every valley shall be filled, and every mountain and hill shall be brought low, and the crooked shall be made straight, and the rough ways shall be made smooth; and all flesh shall see the salvation of God" (Luke 3:1ff.).

A prophet had arisen in Israel.

CHAPTER THREE

The Face of God

Riverside Church in New York City is one of the biggest churches in the USA. It has the biggest carillon of bells in the world, and the nave can seat 2000 comfortably. There are, in addition, 14 kitchens, 8 chapels, a bowling alley, a theater, a radio station, and a gymnasium, as well as many remarkable sculptures and other works of art. It was built by the Rockefellers, but their patronage did not prevent it all going up in flames just before it was due to be opened. Nothing daunted, they built it again, and there it stands above the Hudson, ministering to the complex needs of a great city. When the church was finally opened, Harry Emerson Fosdick, a famous Baptist preacher of the 1920's, was called to be its first minister. At the opening service he stood in the pulpit, at the beginning of his sermon, and gazed at the thousands of people below him and up and around at a building that had cost millions of dollars, and started something like this: "It is strange to remember that all this is built to the honor of a Galilean carpenter who had no place to lay his head." Unfortunately, I have never been able to discover how he continued the sermon, how he dealt with that tantalizing opening contrast between the poor Christ and the Church built by the Rockefeller millions. Christian history is full of such eloquent paradoxes. Preachers like Fosdick are particularly fond of the strange contrast between the one who was born in a stable and had nowhere to lay his head and the conspicuous wealth of many of his later followers. In the name of the poor man of Nazareth riches have been heaped up on earth, and his chief officers have often chosen to reside in palaces. Under the ironic providence of God inflation has happily removed the more glaring aspects of that paradox, though it is still a standard weapon in every village atheist's armory.

I want to begin this chapter by pointing to a less dramatic paradox, though it is deeper and, I think, more significant. It is the fact that in this book I am addressing myself to that part of the educated public which reads theological literature and I am seeking to make a case for the Christian Faith in a way that might appeal to it. The paradox lies more in even attempting such an enterprise than in not succeeding at it, because from the earliest days of the church there has been a tendency for intellectuals to look upon the Christian Faith as contemptuous. Jesus himself recognized this tendency and once prayed in these words: "I thank thee Father, Lord of heaven and earth, that thou didst hide these things from the wise and understanding, and didst reveal them unto babes." Paul pointed out in his letter to the church at Corinth that not many of them were wise or powerful. God seemed to have succeeded in revealing himself only to fools. You'll remember these famous words of Jesus: "Unless you become as little children you shall not enter the kingdom of heaven." What did Jesus mean by setting forth children as examples of faith? Well, he clearly did not mean that we were not to progress beyond the Sunday School in our understanding. He was, I think, drawing our attention to what is perhaps the most attractive characteristic of normal and healthy young children: the fresh and uncomplicated way in which they accept others at face value. As we say today, they don't bring a "hidden agenda" to their estimate of others: they accept them as they are; thus people are able to disclose themselves to them with an uninterpreted directness. You might say they are ripe for revelations, because their vision and understanding are not yet complicated by all the suspicions and disappointments that clutter and complicate our adult response to others. The Gospels tell us that the poor heard Jesus gladly, because they were not defensively guarding some position of their own which he threatened. He came through to them with uninterrupted clarity as he was in himself, whereas the clever immediately tried to figure him out, to prove and test him, and by doing so they missed the revelation. They did not really hear or see what Jesus was in himself. What they got was a Jesus filtered and refracted and edited by their own minds.

There is an interesting similarity here between genius and childlikeness. We are often told, for instance, that the scientific attitude is essentially sceptical and negative, proving by denying. It seems to be the case, however, that the creative geniuses of science arrive at their great discoveries by something closer to a revelatory experience, which often follows a humble waiting for nature to disclose itself to them. The fact remains that it can be very difficult for clever people to come to faith. This is partly, I think, because the intellect is very often critical and negative in its mode of operation, and properly so; but this critical role can be hazardous when we are dealing with the really important things in life. If it becomes fixed and unalterable, the critic misses much. Take, for instance, creative art, as in music or writing. It is often said by artists, somewhat ruefully, that those who can create do so, while those who can't criticize. The role of the artist is creative and affirmative: he sets forth what he sees and hears. He receives what is revealed to him by an indefinable, intuitive process. The critic receives nothing. His task is analytic, corrective, secondary to, and ultimately parasitic upon the original creative act. If his critical faculty is unchecked by awe and humility he can cut the vision to shreds. We need critics to help guard us against the phoney and the second-rate, but they often miss the point completely, and history is filled with the record of their profound mistakes.

Nowhere is this more obvious than in the field of religion. The prophet proclaims a word of God in poetic form, but rather than listen to *what* is said the critic sets out to examine the meter. He misses the message because he's so intent upon analyzing the medium. Some of this is just a bad habit, but much of it is avoidance technique, a diversionary exercise set up to avoid making a decision. Karl Marx and Cardinal Newman were at one in recognizing that life is for action and that intellectuals were past masters at indefinitely postponing action. The mode of action that is appropriate to the revelation of God is faith, but the critical intellect endlessly postpones the decision of faith as it seeks to build a better case for believing. But life is never long enough for this process. As Cardinal Newman put it,

... we shall never have done beginning, if we determine to begin with proof. We shall ever be laying foundations. If we insist on proofs for every thing, we shall never come to action: to act you must assume, and that assumption is faith (*A Grammar of Assent*; South Bend: University of Notre Dame Press, 1979, p. 90).

I have tried in the first two chapters to outline something of this process of searching for proofs. We were left with a hypothesis, a supposition. We cannot break it down any further, though certain people go on anxiously questioning and disputing, searching for the clinching argument. Why is it never found? Why doesn't God make it easier for us to believe by giving us a clear demonstration of his existence? Let me quote from an answer that C. S. Lewis gave to that very question.

As to why God does not make his existence demonstratively clear: are we sure that He is even interested in the kind of Theism which would be a compelled logical assent to a conclusive argument? Are *we* interested in it in personal matters? I demand from my friends a trust in my good faith which is certain without demonstrative proof. It wouldn't be confidence at all if he waited for rigorous proof. Othello believed in Desdemona's innocence when it was proved: but that was too late. 'His praise is lost who stays till all commend'. The magnanimity, the generosity which will trust on a reasonable probability is required of us. But supposing one believed and was wrong after all? Why, then you would have paid the universe a compliment it doesn't deserve. Your error would even so be more interesting and important than the reality. And yet how could that be? How could an idiotic universe have produced creatures whose mere dreams are so much stronger, better, subtler than itself? (quoted in Sheldon Vanauken, *A Severe Mercy*; London: Hodder & Stoughton, 1977, p. 92).

I have always felt the force of the point made in this last sentence by Lewis. Since the object of faith can never be logically demonstrated, you are left with the momentous choice of willing yourself to believe, of making a commitment, of deciding henceforth to act as though God were. Several things have to be said about this "will to believe," as William James described it.

First of all, it is the last ditch into which the believer can be driven by the assaults of unbelief. We are never given in this life the kind of intellectual assurance that is higher than a reasonable probability. Well then, if it comes to that, let us make an act of defiance against those forces in the universe that would persuade us that, ultimately, we come from nothing and go to nothing. Let us with a clear head choose to believe that the universe is not absurd, that it has meaning, and that if it has a meaning there must be somebody to mean it. The cowardly or the careful might reply, "But what if you're wrong?" Well, the answer to that was never given more eloquently than by the Spanish philosopher Miguel de Unamuno: "If we are perishing let us perish resisting. If it is nothingness that awaits us, let us so act that it will be an unjust fate." The act of faith, then, becomes a great gesture of defiance, an act of revolution. We stand up and we refuse to be nothing. We resist. That is the last wall against which the believer can be pushed. Here he stands and begins to fight back.

That gesture of defiance may appeal to something in man's heart, but it is more than an act of romantic desperation. It is a profoundly affirmative act. There is something in human nature and its deepest instincts that revolts against the intellectual vacuum created by atheism. Belief seems to correspond with some of our deepest convictions. Schubert Ogden makes a distinction between what he calls belief in "the top of our mind" and belief in "the bottom of our heart." Our mind may pose as a radical sceptic, but our unexamined assumptions about the goodness of life and its proper values may demonstrate that, in the bottom of our hearts, we believe that life has meaning. The most unsatisfactory thing about atheism is that it is essentially about nothing, whereas in man there seems to be a permanent sympathy with meaning, a need to affirm rather than deny. In other words, the idea that there is a God who gives meaning to life seems to correspond to the way we actually *experience* life. Of course, that statement has to be modified in all sorts of ways to fit individuals. The general point remains that most people throughout most of history have affirmed life and valued it in a way that would be extraordinary if the universe were just an accidental collocation of atoms. It is the universal persistence of this idea of God which most irritates the tiny band of earnest atheists in our society. They make their appeal to the minds of men and women and bid them, in the name of reason, to cast off this error. They would do well to heed some words of Carl Jung:

> Nothing influences our conduct less than do intellectual ideas. But when an idea is the expression of psychic experience which bears fruit in regions as far separated and free from historical relation as East and West, then we must look into the matter closely. For such ideas are present forces that are beyond logical justification and moral sanction; they are always stronger than man and his brain. Man believes indeed that he moulds these ideas, but in reality they mould him and make him their unwitting mouthpiece (*Modern Man in Search of a Soul*; London: Routledge and Kegan Paul, 1973, p. 48).

So this apparently quixotic act of defiance which we call faith has the paradoxical effect of putting us in touch with the deepest part of our own nature. It's as though we had some hitherto undiscovered secret of balance within us which is not discovered until we do the apparently daring thing and step out on to the high wire. The analogy is apt enough, for the experience of faith, like swimming or riding a bike or walking on a tightrope, brings no advance guarantee with it. If you wait for the conclusive proof you'll wait forever, and in vain. Now, I've offered a few analogies from our experience with various activities that require us to trust in an inner aptitude we cannot discover until we actually do the thing we are afraid to do. You all know the legendary fatuity of the mother who said her little Johnny was not going to be allowed into the water till he learned to swim. That's a partial analogy of faith. And C. S. Lewis quoted examples of a trust that came only when it was too late because it demanded assurance in advance. These help us a little to understand the nature of the mysterious activity called faith in God, but they get us only part of the way. Helpful though these analogies are, they are at least dealing with empirical realities like bicycles and swimming pools and other human beings. God, we say, is not real in the same way. Learning to ride a bike may call for a kind of trust, but we are not asked to put our trust in an invisible bike. Trusting one's friends may sometimes call for courage, but our friends are *there*. Faith in God is unique because it is, apparently, faith *that* he is there against all the appearances to the contrary. The position, however, is not quite so desperate as that. I talked in the first two chapters about Revelation and about a remarkable class of people through whom, it is claimed, God has spoken. One level of trust, therefore, is trust in them, belief that they are not mad or liars. Jung came close to this mysterious phenomenon when he talked about ideas that mold man and make him their unwitting mouthpiece. It is here that we must make ourselves capable of some of that childlikeness that I talked of earlier.

What do we do, for instance, when we read the words of the prophets? Few of us, I suspect, listen to them as the word of God. Instead, we transpose them and seek to evaluate them as the subjective experience of the prophet. We seek to account for them not with reference to what the prophet claims is their origin, but with reference to our complicated reaction to them. We "naturalize" them, find an explanation of them on the plane with which we are most familiar. So we come up with a psychological explanation which safely insulates us from the fire that is burning behind the prophet. In fact, we interpret it away. Isn't this true? Don't we bring to all this strange activity a whole rationalistic apparatus that effectively closes us off from the approach of revelation? This is what the dominating tendency in biblical interpretation does. It does not allow itself to confront that to which the prophet refers because it is busily engaged in locating the prophet in his psychological, sociological, and historical context. It unearths a massive number of facts about the prophet and his day but it often avoids meeting the living God who addresses us through his servant the prophet. On a more homely level, this is what many people do when they listen to sermons, especially if they are themselves preachers! They rarely open their ears to hear what the Lord says to them because they are critically engaged in evaluating the sermon. I have found this a great difficulty myself. When I read the account of John the Baptist, for instance, I come up to a tremendous gulf between experience and understanding. John appears, according to Luke, at a specific point in history:

In the fifteenth year of the reign of Tiberius Caesar, Pontius Pilate being governor of Judea, and Herod being tetrarch of Galilee, and his brother Philip tetrarch of the region of Ituraea and Trachonitis, and Lysanias tetrarch of Abilene, in the high-priesthood of Annas and Caiaphas, the word of God came to John the son of Zechariah in the wilderness (Luke 3:1-2).

The first part of this we can cope with. It establishes John in a particular historical context. We know, for instance, about Tiberius, the infamous Roman emperor. He was a dour and capable man who began his reign well enough. Soon, however, he became obsessive and bitter and the final years of his reign were darkened with cruelty and corruption. Just before John came forth from the desert, Tiberius had withdrawn to the Island of Capri, leaving the administration of the Empire in the hands of his unscrupulous and odious favorite, Sejanus, who later overreached himself and was assassinated. So these words "in the fifteenth year of the reign of Tiberius Caesar" remind us of the darkness and corruption and political chaos of the Roman Empire. "Herod being tetrarch of Galilee, and his brother Philip tetrarch of the region of Ituraea and Trachonitis, and Lysanias tetrarch of Abilene." These words remind us of another fact, the domination of the Holy Land by a pagan power which trampled upon its ancient privileges. The Romans divided the Holy Land into four regions and placed over them puppet princes, "tetrarchs," most of whom were moral degenerates and administratively incompetent. The ancient people of Israel were humbled by a corrupt and overweening foreign power. "In the high-priesthood of Annas and Caiaphas." This is further evidence of the sorry state of Israel. Not only were their political rulers imposed upon them, so were their spiritual rulers. Annas was high priest from AD 6 to AD 15, when he was deposed by the Roman governor. Caiaphas was made high priest by the Romans in AD 18 and ruled to AD 36. In fact, Annas was always the power behind the throne, even after he was deposed. Caiaphas was his son-in-law. Luke was right in his rather strange claim that the high priest was not Caiaphas but Annas-and-Caiaphas. It was a long time ago, of course, and the details are exotic and breathe over us the faint smell of an ancient corruption, but it's history, however disputed the details may be.

What can we make of the next claim: "the word of God came to John the son of Zechariah in the wilderness"? I know I'm laboring heavily over this, but I want to reach a certain point, a certain recognition. Can we somehow open ourselves to the fact, not that a wild man from a hippy-commune in the Judean wilderness dreamed up a religious happening out of his own fevered mind, but that God's word, his spirit, entered into John and sent him forth on a mission? I know we are inescapably tied up in metaphors here. Forget them. Can you grasp the fact that God *acted* in John? Can you bring yourself to believe that what happened then was traceable only back to God? What you are called upon to do here is to open yourself to a *particular* action of God. Having made the leap toward a generalized belief in God, it may not be too difficult to conceive of a general sense in which God is ultimately in some sort of control. The technical name for that conviction is Deism. It postulates a god who does not interfere in particular ways but only according to general, unalterable laws. That is not biblical religion, it is not the truth that revelation claims to know. What we call revelation is the claim that God is active in quite specific and particular ways. That he inspires and sends the prophets and that when we hear them we hear him, clothed in their utterance. It is true that the divine utterance is in some sense modified and qualified by its human mediation, but that is not the main truth, though it is the truth that modern theology fastens on and rarely progresses from. I want you to grasp something enormous and liberating. C. H. Dodd called it the "scandal of particularity": God approaches us by mediating himself through the minds, hearts, and lips of men and women *to whom he comes*. "The word of God came to John the son of Zechariah in the wilderness," the Bible tells us, and that's what it means. What we have is a going forth of God into what comes to us as human speech. John has to be understood, therefore, against the tempestuous background of Jewish prophecy. It was in dark and depressing days that God's word came to John, as once it had come to the Old Testament prophets, speaking through them to Israel, warning, threatening, pleading. There had been no prophet in Israel for hundreds of years. The word of God seemed to have left Israel. The old vision had faded, the fire had burned low, when forth from the desert came John, preaching. He began his ministry about the year AD 27, when the passage we've been looking at is approximately dated. Grasp that. The word of God is heard again at a precise moment of time. The word "preaching" comes from the Greek word for herald, someone who came before the visit of a ruler to announce his approach, his advent, and to order preparations for his arrival. John announced a coming and he demanded preparation. The preparation he demanded was repentance. By this he meant a turning away from sin and a turning toward God.

"The word of God came unto John the son of Zechariah in the wilderness. And he came into all the region round Jordan, preaching the baptism of repentance for the remission of sins." Some responded. More were infuriated, because the people of Judea had little sense of their own sinfulness, no notion that they needed to repent. John called them to a radical self-examination, and he quoted an ancient prophecy from Isaiah. "The voice of one crying in the wilderness, Make ye ready the way of the Lord, make his paths straight. Every valley shall be filled, and every mountain and hill shall be brought low; and the crooked shall become straight, and the rough ways smooth; and all flesh shall *see* the salvation of God." The passage had originally referred to the return of Judah from exile in Babylon, and paints a picture of a royal progress through the wilderness. But John used the passage to point to a much more significant return, the return of God to his people in *person*, in the person of his Messiah. Just as a road had to be made in the desert for that first approach, so a way had to be prepared in the lives and hearts of people for the approach of the Lord's anointed. The crooked had to be made straight: all departures from the moral law of God had to be straightened out. All pride and arrogance and self-satisfaction had to be brought low, and all self-will broken down. So John the herald went forth to prepare people for the one greater than he who was to follow. Some heard him gladly and repented of their sins and were baptized to show the sincerity of their conversion. Many muttered and plotted against him. John, like all the prophets, was to be rejected by men. As you know, he was executed. His role was magnificent, but limited. He steps on the stage of history to utter a mysterious prologue which he himself probably did not entirely understand, and then he departs in violence, testimony to the strange law that compels human nature to silence the word of God when it goes forth, either by the quick death of sword or hammer blow or by the slow death of a thousand qualifications. But let us leave John here, at the high noon of his ministry, a strange, harsh, compelling figure, crying, crying to men to prepare the way of the Lord.

Paradoxically, I want to end this section with a prologue. Theologians call the first fourteen verses of John's Gospel "prologue." The simplest way to see these verses is as a prologue to the rest of the Gospel, but the word has a more profound, less literary significance. In a real sense, for the first great Christian theologians everything before Christ was "prologue," was *before the Word* itself was uttered in flesh. Everything, including the whole of history, was prologue, for in Christ the meaning and heart of all things was revealed, not this time in the sundry and various guises it had assumed in the words of the prophets, but in the very flesh of our own humanity. To enter into the meaning of that tremendous prologue we have to seek to enter the heart of God. Prophetic religion, remember, claims that what we have in prophecy is a glimpse into the very heart of God.

The drama and pathos of God's overture to humanity before Christ is poignantly captured in these fourteen verses, fourteen verses of the simplest Greek ever written. They tell of a time beyond time when God was all, and when the Word that later came to his servants the prophets was with God, was God himself. All things were made by this same Word that was later to break into the hearts of a few, a very few, who were disposed to receive it. He was the source of all life. And that life was the light, the soul, the very reason of man. But it was as if the flame were to hold itself aloof from and independent of the candle that gave it life. It claimed to burn by its own brightness, it knew not its own origin. So that flame burned in a strange darkness of incomprehension. And here John uses a deliberately ambiguous word. The light, he says, shines in the darkness, and the darkness does not "apprehend" it. That is to say, it does not capture it, put it out, overcome it; but it is also to say it does not understand it, make it out, make it its own. And then John the Baptist is mentioned as the type and representative of all the prophets to whom this light came and was understood. John, like all the prophets, bore witness to the source and origin of all things, to the light that lightens all men.

Then there occur some of the most poignant verses in the whole Bible, filled with all the ancient sorrow of God. This Word, this light that came to prophet and seer, had from the beginning been in the world, the world that he had made, but the world knew him not. He came, endlessly and everlastingly he came to his own, and his own received him not. Some, of course, did receive him. In every generation some are genuine children of God. To these God had always come, finding an entrance, a way to plead with those who received him not. And then is made the staggering claim. This history of divine imploring was a failure. The ancient patience of God was unrewarded by any significant realization on the part of his children. The flame burned proudly in its own light and God lay still concealed. So God himself enters his own created order, not this time indirectly, not by the ambiguous mediation of words but in very flesh. God does not take flesh as a temporary device to capture attention, God *becomes* flesh. Not by inspiring in a special way some meek and holy man, like John, who was born of the will of human flesh by the action of a human father. No, but by the action and initiative of the will of God. The Word, John tells us, the Word became flesh and took up a temporary abode with us—the word almost means "camped" among us. We have heard the words so often that we have become anesthetized against the shock of the claim that is being made. This is not just another claim about an inspired prophet through whom God speaks in a uniquely eloquent way. It is not a claim about a man of unique holiness in whom it was possible to catch traces of the divine presence. The claim is much more scandalous than that. The claim is that this *is* God, at last, face to face with his own. As it is put in the letter to the Hebrews,

God, who at sundry times and in diverse manners spake in time past unto the fathers by the prophets, hath in these last days spoken unto us by his Son (1:1-2).

It is the central claim of the Christian revelation. If it is not true, then our faith is vain and we are found liars before men. How did this claim come to be made about Jesus of Nazareth?

CHAPTER FOUR

Puzzling Reflections in a Mirror

M ost people come to religious faith by means of some sort of inheritance. They may, for instance, be born into a religious family and part of their early nurture includes the absorption of a set of beliefs which are handed on to them. They inherit a whole series of attitudes and convictions, much in the way that the children of the rich inherit wealth which they have not themselves earned. There are, of course, enormous differences both in the way this religious training is given and in the seriousness with which it is absorbed. Sometimes it lasts for life without interruption or serious questioning. Sometimes it is broken by youthful revolt and taken up again later in life as a conscious choice. W. H. Auden described this contrast as "believing still" or "believing again." Even those who have not received this early religious nurture but who become believers as a result of conscious choice as adults are still, in some sense, inheritors. They find faith because they have come into contact with the church or with religious believers or because of their reading on the subject. I am not saying, of course, that there is not also some divine prompting, some mysterious action of God in their lives which draws them toward faith. Nevertheless, it is true that the formation of faith and its mature articulation usually owe a great deal to others who have maintained the inheritance of faith. There have been some who have been converted because they have read the New Testament for the first time. Even this, however, does not contradict what I am saying, because the New Testament is itself part of this inheritance that has been handed down. The New

Testament is the beginning of the church's collective memory. The important point to grasp in all this is that most of us have our faith, in some sense, at second hand. It is mediated to us. There is a middleman between us and its origin. And there is great danger in this. It can mean that what we believe is a set of articles of belief, a number of propositions. We believe, not God but the creed. We trust, not in Jesus but what the church teaches about Jesus. And this can become pathological. A kind of mind can develop which makes the words about God and Jesus as important or more important than the personal beings to whom they refer. Part of the problem here lies in our quest for a kind of absolute security. This is an innate craving in human beings, and it finds its satisfaction in the various kinds of fundamentalism that characterize human history. You can absolutize the infallible church or a political party or a historical theory. That's one danger, and it is significant that in these dangerous and uncertain times there has been a resurgence of fundamentalism throughout the world and throughout human society, both secular and religious. It was this impulse which led Aaron to fashion a golden calf for the Israelites who were tired of the mystery and elusiveness of the God who had led them forth from Egypt. "Behold your god, O Israel." Part of the danger, as I've said, lies in the human need for security, for some kind of authority that won't let us down, but part of the danger lies elsewhere.

This kind of overbelief in the verbal articulation of religious mysteries is really a symptom of a subtle if unacknowledged lack of really fundamental belief. We're not really sure if we believe in God, so we compensate by believing lots of things *about* him. And who can blame us? We need something to hold on to. Deep down we are uncertain about the meaning of existence, and since we don't or can't really believe in God we raise up a whole series of structures on which we pin our longings and fears and hopes. By one of those ironies of which history is full, religion itself becomes a substitute for God. Indeed, it becomes the enemy of God. There is a scandalous paradox at the heart of the Christian Faith because the record shows that it was in God's name that God was crucified. "We have a law, and by that law he ought to die, because he made himself out to be the Son of God." Men preferred their traditions *about* God to God himself, so that when he came they could not recognize him. And is this not due to a fundamental atheism in us? We won't, in fact, allow God to be God. We want him away in the heavens so that we can organize things our way, including what may be said about him. Jesus told a parable about a king who went on a journey and left his kingdom in charge of his subjects. He sent emissaries back to collect tribute, but they were put to death. So he sent his son. There might have been a mistake made about the other emissaries. Surely there could be none about his son? But there was. Or was it a mistake? Anyway, the son, too, was put to death. It is the ancient story, the story told in John's prologue. "He came to his own, and his own received him not." They never do. This is obviously true in the moral sphere. We don't want God to come among us because his demands are unacceptable. We have his kingdom nicely organized to our own benefit, and we do not want to listen to his pleas for justice and righteousness. But we don't want God's interference in the intellectual sphere, either. We don't want him interrupting our theories. We don't want our assumptions disturbed. We want to remain in control of the action. That's why we like words *about* God. Them we can manipulate and rearrange and play games with. We can't do that with God. That's why we prefer a theory about God to God himself.

So, you see, there is a great obstacle in our way as we try to find God. Most of us don't find *him* at all. We find that we are traveling through a great swamp of words and theories and concepts and ideas, with all sorts of hucksters established in business in swampland, living in little reed huts stuck up on stilts, crying to us to buy one of their little residences. There's the light-and-airy liberal residence with lovely views and no foundations. There's the solid fundamentalist longhut, made out of packed mud so thick that you can't see out of it. There's the elegant and vividly decorated catholic cabin which requires a lot of extra maintenance. And there's an interesting outfit called the radical alternative who don't believe in huts at all and spend most of their time trying to bomb the others out of existence. Most of us fit into one or other of these little schemes. Occasionally we swap dwellings. Sometimes we get so tired of the hostilities between the swamp dwellers that we turn around and go back to whatever Egypt we came from.

Is it possible, then, to outflank the swamp? Can we, somehow, avoid the middlemen who come between us and what we are looking for? Must we forever be looking back at Jesus through the wrong end of the telescope? Well, I don't think it is entirely possible, but it is worth a try. I myself need to attempt it because I have come increasingly to realize that, like the man who went down from Jerusalem to Jericho, I have fallen among thieves. As I look back over the years I have been studying theology, I realize that much of what I have studied has been a barrier between me and Jesus. Oh, I don't mean that anyone has set out to deceive me, or that there has been a conscious lack of sincerity in those whom I have studied. No, I feel instead that the whole theological enterprise has become a kind of substitutionary rite which works to keep you from meeting the living Jesus. For instance, at college I almost never read the Scriptures (except in chapel, which didn't count) without at the same time filtering them through innumerable commentaries. Everything came interpreted or explained or paraphrased or elucidated. What I got was what certain scholars made of what certain other scholars had made of the meaning of Jesus. Which is where we started in this chapter: everything about Jesus is strained through a thick mesh of commentary and interpretation and counter-interpretation. It's a bit like trying to communicate with someone sitting silently in the far corner of a vast hall which is filled with thousands of angry disputants all claiming to represent the true meaning of the compelling but inaccessible figure in the distance. What I long to do is to get back to that original encounter between God and man that set the whole interpretative process in motion. Because this is where all genuine religion starts: with revelation, with a moment of real encounter between the human and the divine. That, of course, is where we stumble. It is the preciseness of it that frightens us. We can cope with generalities. It is the particular that scares us or offends us: the idea that this man or woman had, at a specific moment in time, an encounter with the living God. Of course, accounts of these things confront us on the pages of the Scriptures, but we have long since grown used to the suggestion that they are simply a primitive way of speaking about something vague and general and unexceptionable. So we trade that ancient dry land for the modern swamp of interpretation. I want to try to get some sort of foothold on that dry land, but I want to take a very rapid flight over it first to get some idea of its extent.

If one were to open the New Testament for the first time and start reading Matthew's Gospel and then read right on to the end of the Book of Revelation, one could be excused for thinking that here we have some sort of developing story in various literary forms. To a certain extent that's true. The Gospels give us some kind of chronological account of Jesus' life. The Acts of the Apostles describes the trials and successes of the early church. And the letters obviously illustrate, often with baffling opacity, the life of the scattered Christian communities. The Book of Revelation, to conclude, is clearly written by some early Christian prophet in a time of struggle and persecution. That's a possible way to see it all, of course, but it does not reflect what we know about the emergence of the different elements themselves. We know, for instance, that the earliest parts of what we now call the New Testament were the letters of Paul. They provide us with very strong historical evidence of the preaching of the church not much more than twenty years after the death of Jesus. They reflect a period of great missionary expansion and they afford us glimpses of the fundamental claim of the earliest Christian evangelists. The Acts of the Apostles, though it was written as the second volume of Luke's account of the Christian movement, covers the same period in retrospect. This period of expansion was followed by a period of conflict and persecution which climaxed in the year AD 64 when Rome was burned to the ground and the Christians provided a convenient scapegoat. It is probable that First Peter and the Letter to the Hebrews were written at this time, reflecting, as they do, an era of persecution. Revelation, though written much later, also reflects a period of persecution and assumes that suffering is the normal vocation of Christians. We can be fairly certain that during this period the original eyewitnesses of Christ's ministry were dying off and that this gave the stimulus to the formation of what we call the Gospels. The earliest was Mark's, and it, too, reflects the period of persecution which the church was undergoing.

It must be fairly obvious from this brief summary of the period that the first Christian preaching was not an exposition or interpretation of the New Testament. It was not dependent upon written sources. What it first preached and taught with all the passion of firsthand testimony later became our Scripture, and by that time a subtle transformation had taken place. The first preaching had all the immediacy of personal testimony: dying men were preaching to dying men, and they were pointing to one whom they proclaimed was the Prince of Life. Men responded as to something living and immediately accessible, and that accounted for the fantastic success of the first evangelists. After that springtime of faith a third element intruded: the words which had been used to mediate the reality of the One who was in their midst. Now, words on a page can be used in many ways. They can be used as a means whereby the living Word is communicated, or as a device for avoiding him. In our search for dry land, can we get back behind the words to the experience they express? Can we get behind the words to the Word? I want to try.

What would you say, I wonder, if I told you about a man who had never read the Gospels, never entered a church, never known Jesus in life, but who claimed that he had been met by him after his death? When we read Paul's testimony we come to grips with the real claims of a real man. Unlike us, Paul had inherited no vague tradition about Jesus. He was, as he reminds us again and again, a persecutor of the church. Jesus was dead. The Gospels had not been written, though doubtless Paul had heard the claims that were made about Jesus. There is no evidence that he had ever met Jesus while he was alive. But something happened to Paul, and Paul is quite precise about it. He does not say that he was gradually persuaded by a systematic investigation of the evidence. He does not point to any human intermediaries. Quite the reverse. In one of his earliest letters, the Letter to the Galatians, written about AD 55, he tells us that what he learned about Christ he learned from Christ—who had been dead twenty-five years!

> I would have you know, brethren, that the gospel which was preached by me is not man's gospel. For I did not

receive it from man, nor was I taught it, *but it came through a revelation of Jesus Christ.*

He alludes to his experience on the road to Damascus and says that after this revelation he "did not confer with flesh and blood" nor did he go to Jerusalem to confer with the apostles, but that he went away into Arabia. It was only after three years, three years after his conversion, that he went to Jerusalem to meet Peter and the other apostles. This is one of the insistent themes of Paul's message. His is not a human gospel. Christian preachers do not preach themselves nor their own cleverness. They preach what has been revealed to them, and what has been revealed to them is that Jesus is Lord and Savior. Now we must make a valiant attempt not to slip back into the swamp by seeking to *explain* what Paul says. Can we not let him have his say and entertain the possibility that he is speaking the sober truth? Do we not have here one of those fontal moments in religious history when you get back behind all subsequent interpretation and come up against the original encounter between God and man? Paul claims that he had an experience of God which led him into the desert for three years; here he meditated and learned from God without human intermediary. That may be straightforward enough. There is plenty of that kind of thing in religious history. What is completely new here is that that primal experience of God which Paul had was at the same time an experience of a man who had been crucified in recent memory. When Paul talks about it, his language constantly slides back and forth between God and Christ. He is not using language with any theological stringency. He is not working out a theory of Christ. He is describing an experience, and in so doing he is using language that defines Jesus Christ as being what God is.

> He is the image of the invisible God, the first-born of all creation; for in him all things were created, in heaven and on earth, visible and invisible, whether thrones or dominions or principalities or authorities—all things were created through him and for him. He is before all things, and in him all things hold together. He is the head of the body, the church; he is the beginning, the first-born from

the dead, that in everything he might be pre-eminent.
For in him all the fulness of God was pleased to dwell,
and through him to reconcile to himself all things, whether
on earth or in heaven, making peace by the blood of his
cross (Colossians 1:15-20).

And remember, all this is found in the earliest documents of
the Christian scriptorium. It is often said by a certain type of
scholar that this high view of Christ was the result of a natural
process of elaboration upon an earlier simplicity. The fact is
that we find it at the very beginning of the Christian story. It
is *Christ* that is being preached, and preached in a way that
implies, where it does not state explicitly, an identity between
God and Christ. Paul's preaching was the result of an independent revelation, but it does not contradict the preaching of
Peter as reported by Luke in the Acts of the Apostles.

"You denied the Holy and Righteous One, and asked for
a murderer to be granted to you, and killed the Author
of life, whom God raised from the dead. To this we are
witnesses. . . . Repent therefore and turn again, that your
sins may be blotted out, that times of refreshing may come
from the presence of the Lord, and that he may send the
Christ appointed for you, Jesus . . ." (Acts 3:14ff.).

Peter, like Paul, is preaching from experience. He is bearing witness, as he himself says. It did not occur to them to work
out the theoretical implications of what they were saying, and
at this stage I am not concerned to do so either. There is little
evidence that they offered much in the way of biographical
information about Jesus. The summary of their message was
that this Jesus whom they had crucified was the Holy One of
God, whom God had raised from the dead and who was now
accessible to all men by repentance and faith in his name. Characteristic of the message is this almost uncomprehending identification of God and Christ. Christ has for them the value of
God. He is the object of their worship and self-surrender. For
Paul he has become the very principle of life itself: "I live, yet
not I; Christ liveth in me."

At this stage in Christian history the apostles are not concerned to contend for the status and meaning of words as they express the meaning and nature of Christ. They are not aware of the problems that are being created for the more theoretical minds that are to follow. They have no apparent concern for the internal arithmetic of the Godhead. Like men possessed, they are desperate to bring as many as they can into a relationship with Jesus. But Jesus is dead! No, he is not dead; he *died*. It is possible, apparently, to know him now, and for those who do, knowing becomes a fact so overwhelming as to render all other facts insignificant.

> Whatever gain I had, I counted as loss for the sake of Christ. Indeed I count everything as loss because of the surpassing worth of knowing Christ Jesus my Lord. For his sake I have suffered the loss of all things, and count them as refuse, in order that I may gain Christ and be found in him . . . that I may know him and the power of his resurrection, and may share his sufferings, becoming like him in his death, that if possible I may attain the resurrection from the dead (Philippians 3:7ff.).

What kind of talk is this? It is clearly not abstract, general talk about the meaning of things. It is specific talk about a particular, personal experience of an overwhelming relationship. It is absolute language, the language of total surrender. To me it indicates either that Paul was insane or that he had had an untranslatable experience of God in Christ. That, I think, is still the choice. You cannot pretend that Paul did not mean to say what he in fact did say. There is hardly any doubt about what Paul said! Of course, he makes no attempt to work out any kind of systematic account of the nature of Christ. He hasn't time, for one thing. When every minute of your life is spent in attempting to share with people the extraordinary richness of a personal companionship with the everlasting God, made known to you by the supernatural revelation of that God in the risen person of Jesus Christ, you don't have time to figure out all the theoretical implications. Later that would have to be done by the church in order to safeguard the integrity of the revelation. Well, was Paul mad? He was certainly accused of it by the Roman governor Festus. "Paul, you are mad; your great learning is turning you mad," he said to him at his trial before King Agrippa. Paul's reply seems sane enough: "I am not mad, most excellent Festus, but I am speaking the sober truth. For the king knows about these things, and to him I speak freely; for I am persuaded that none of these things has escaped his notice, for this was not done in a corner" (Acts 26:24-26). Mad or not, he was extraordinarily successful in what he set out to do. The Christian movement experienced fantastic growth, which has continued down the ages and continues still. And the growth is based upon the same claim. The thing that baffles outsiders is how it is done.

How does the listener make the leap to an agreement and correspondence with the extraordinary claim that is being made? After all, the claim cannot be proved, it cannot be demonstrated logically. All that logic can do is dispute about the nature of the claim that is made: did Paul believe that Jesus was God, for instance? If we get enmeshed in that area we have fallen for an attractive deceit. What Paul wanted was actual, living surrender to Jesus Christ. He wanted his hearers to give their lives away to Jesus, not become protagonists in a debate about his metaphysical status. If you are prepared to die for someone, it does not really matter what speculative interpretation you would put upon your act. Faith is action, and of course it is faith that bridges this mysterious gap between the claim made and the assent given. Faith is the only faculty which can achieve correspondence with God, and it lies latent within us, waiting to be called forth, waiting to answer the call. Nothing else can account for the mysterious success of the Christian Faith than the reality of Christ himself. He is the third person in any evangelistic enterprise. He is the presence that stands behind the inconspicuous person of the speaker of the momentous word. He is the force that fuses its way through the evangelist's stumbling affirmations. Any evangelist knows this. He knows that something comes through him, though it is not from him. It is not a human activity in its entirety. There is a mysterious but certain extra factor which is the reality of Christ himself. This is why Paul was successful, because what he said was verified in the experience and in the response of his listeners—not to him as such, but to the One who called them in the very depths of their own beings. Paul knew this, which is why he said in some famous words in the Letter to the Romans:

> Do not say in your heart, "Who will ascend into heaven?" (that is, to bring Christ down) or "Who will descend into the abyss?" (that is, to bring Christ up from the dead). But what does it say? The word is near you, on your lips and in your heart (that is, the word of faith which we preach); because if you confess with your lips that Jesus is Lord and believe in your heart that God raised him from the dead, you will be saved (Romans 10:6ff.).

It is an ancient biblical truth that "there are two that bear witness." Whenever the word is preached, whenever testimony is borne, there are two witnesses who speak. One is obviously the human witness, the oftentimes stumbling and uneloquent evangelist. The other is the Holy Spirit of God, giving his inward assurance, bearing his witness within the soul. It is this fact that gives evangelists their assurance. After all, they bear witness, on the historical level, to certain facts that can never be conclusively argued to an unanswerable conclusion. The very facts themselves are ambiguous and capable of many interpretations. The Christian always makes part of his appeal to history, but that appeal is always balanced by what Bishop Gore called "the appeal to a continuous spiritual experience of need and satisfaction." He goes on to say that the Christian "has expected the Spirit of God, working in the hearts of men, to generate such an inward disposition and experience as to make the testimony to past events credible and certain to their minds." Something answers from within, or doesn't. After all, our Lord himself warned us that no external event, however dramatic, could force from the beholders that mysterious disposition called faith. "If they hear not Moses and the prophets, neither will they be persuaded though one rose from the dead." St. James was alluding to an aspect of the same phenomenon when he told his readers that "the devils believe, and tremble." It is possible to accept the "facts" and nothing else.

I said earlier in this chapter that the "facts" can be a problem for us: we can be so insistent upon our commitment to them that we miss their meaning. They become propositions in our creed, a dead thing, rather than the shared memories of a personal experience, a living thing. Or they become historical data which elicit no inward correspondence, no private commitment. There is a good example of this kind of thing in the sixth chapter of Mark's Gospel in the account of the miraculous feeding of the five thousand. Jesus had taken his disciples away to a lonely place for a well-earned rest. Mark tells us that they were so busy ministering to the needs of the multitude that they did not even have time to eat. There was, however, to be no escape from the multitude that thronged around Jesus wherever he went. As he taught them, the hour grew late. Finally, in exasperation the disciples came to him and asked him to send the crowd away, in order that they might buy food for themselves in the villages round about. There was no attempt to disguise their irritation. When Jesus suggested that *they* provide the crowd with something to eat, their ill temper swelled into a sarcastic retort. "Shall we go and buy two hundred denarii worth of bread, and give it to them to eat?" That was about a year's wages for a laborer. It was meant to be a very cutting jibe. With impatient authority, Jesus sent them to find out how much food there was among the multitude, and they came back with five loaves and two fish. Taking what was available, Jesus fed the whole multitude, using the disciples to distribute the food. No attempt is made to say *how* it was done, and there is no suggestion in the narrative that the crowd knew the miraculous nature of their evening meal. What is certain, however, is that the disciples knew what had happened, had followed the event step by step. With mysterious urgency Jesus sent the disciples away by boat, possibly to keep the nature of the event secret. Later when they were facing difficulties, rowing against a fierce headwind, he came to them, walking on the water. Mark tells us that they were utterly astounded, "for they did not understand about the loaves, but their hearts were hardened." Now, the disciples certainly realized that the multitude had been fed, but they had failed to grasp that this event pointed beyond itself to the secret of Jesus' person. Because they were not truly open to God's revelatory activity in Jesus, they had missed the real significance of the event. For them it was only a wonder, a mighty deed.

Later I want to examine the vexed subject of the miraculous in the life and work of Jesus; now I want only to point out that it was never enough to accept the miracles at their face value. They had to be interpreted or read if their significance was not to be lost either in the kind of hysteria that often accompanied observance of the power of Jesus, or in the matter-of-fact, "so what?" kind of attitude that might characterize certain connoisseurs of the paranormal.

The miracles of Jesus are also parables, events which are not immediately self-explanatory. There is a momentous ambivalence about Jesus and his words and works. It is easy to read the printout of events on a surface level, while losing altogether the real encounter that is going on. In other words, while the concrete, historical side of Christianity is important, and while the Christian always makes his appeal to facts, the historical and the factual are always ambiguous; they are always in some sense interpreted by the person's inner disposition. The record states that it was ever thus. Those who heard Jesus were either offended by him, because they thought they knew him: " 'Is not this the carpenter, the son of Mary and brother of James and Joses and Judas and Simon, and are not his sisters here with us?' And they took offense at him." Or they conceived a thoughtless and superficial enthusiasm for him that was entirely based on their own needs: "You seek me, not because you saw signs, but because you ate your fill of the loaves." If the facts concerning Jesus are so prone to ambiguity and misunderstanding, are we wise to lay so much stress upon them? St. Paul said, after all, that though we once knew Jesus "after the flesh," now we know him so no longer. Paul, as I tried to show in a very cursory way, is so captivated by the Christ of Glory who appeared to him after the Resurrection that he seems to pay hardly any attention to the Jesus of history. Need we, then? If the important reality is the living Christ of today who can be known now, what need have we of the earthly Christ whose glory was veiled even from his closest followers? Did he not himself tell Mary Magdalene not to cling to him in the Resurrection garden? Is there not, then, a danger that we'll lose the important fact of the present reality of Christ if we pay too much attention to the Christ of the Gospels?

Well, there is much force in the thinking that lies behind these questions and there have been profound Christian thinkers who have answered resoundingly that it is the living Christ of today who matters. Kierkegaard's prophetic denunciation of the mediocrity and formalism of the church of his day was based on an awareness that the Christ of his day was a beautifully embalmed corpse entombed in a book. No longer was he allowed to flame out in anger at his bourgeois followers. That divine insanity was now carefully institutionalized in the locked ward of the Christian liturgy. In our own day the German theologian Bultmann has made a similar protest, though his motives seem to be a curious mixture of passionate longing to invite men and women to a living relationship with Christ crucified today, and intellectual embarrassment at the miraculous nature of the Gospel records. Nevertheless, I believe that we must reject this apparently attractive truncation of the Christian witness. I have tried to show that the prophetic and biblical revelation of God is bound up with the conviction that God acts through specific persons and shows us what is permanently true by this interaction with history. The revelation is never congealed into a set of abstractions which are then liberated from the vehicle that bore them. The interaction is a permanent mode of God's dealings with us. The word of God is alive and active in the Sacred Scriptures. They are not ruins of purely archaeological interest. They are a permanent medium of revelation. To affirm this staggering fact one does not need to be a literalist, according to each word and letter and paragraph an undifferentiated significance. That is really a kind of semantic idolatry. God has borne his witness through the stumbling and often intractable material of human hearts and minds, but his witness has been effective and still has power to convict and convert. As Bishop Gore put it,

> . . . the whole continuous spiritual appeal of Christianity to the hearts and consciences of men rests upon, or is bound up with, a specific witness borne by certain original eye-witnesses to certain events. The inward assurance is made to rest upon facts. It is because the asserted facts are largely supernatural or miraculous, and because so much of spiritual consequence is made to turn upon

them—the whole question, in fact, of God's redemptive purpose—that the Christian records have been, especially in recent times, the subjects of sharply critical examination and many very radical and very different reconstructions (*Belief in God*; London: Murray, 1921, p. 173).

This brings us immediately up against an important question to which we must attempt an answer: how trustworthy are the Gospel narratives as records of fact? My own answer to that question is that they are broadly trustworthy so long as we do not demand from them anything approaching literal infallibility. Let me give an example which may indicate something of my own attitude. The feeding of the five thousand is the one miracle which is found in all four Gospels. I see no reason to doubt that it is a genuine historical record, no matter what modifications we might feel it proper to place upon the details. (For instance, I think it matters very little to the meaning of the story if the arithmetic is not entirely accurate.) Mark, however, provides an account of a second miracle on a similar scale, the feeding of the four thousand. Mark's account is repeated by Matthew, though neither Luke nor John mentions it. There are differences in detail in the two Markan accounts, and there are perfectly respectable scholars who accept the second feeding as a genuine historical record of a separate event. Other scholars, however, are more inclined to believe that the second Markan account is simply a different version of a single event. Mark heard two versions and concluded that they referred to two different episodes, and reported accordingly. The technical name for this is a "doublet." Now, I believe that Christians are free to accept either approach, though I incline to the second theory and think the account of the feeding of the four thousand is probably a doublet of the other miracle. That is an example of the kind of literary problem that the Gospels often present. The important thing to grasp, however, is that there is very strong evidence indeed that Jesus performed a major miracle of "materialization." Of course, there are many today who will repudiate this, not because they can prove that the account is not genuine as a historical record but because they do not believe such a miracle could occur anywhere, at any time, under any circumstance. I shall discuss the problem

presented by the miraculous element in the Gospels in a moment. Meanwhile it is important to recognize that the fundamental objection to this miracle is philosophical, not historical.
We can concede, I think, that in the formation of the record
as we have it a certain amount of entirely natural and predictable overlapping has occurred, as well as a good deal of edi-
torial rearranging of the material. We need not expect from
the Gospel records an absolutely accurate chronological sequence, and we don't need it anyway. What we have are trustworthy memories of the significant highlights of our Lord's
earthly life, composed thirty or forty years after his death, based
on eyewitness accounts. We ought also to remember the extraordinary trustworthiness of primitive memory and oral tradition in an era when written records were few. (A modern
example of a similar process is recorded in Arthur Haley's book
Roots, which traces his search for his own West African
forebears.)

Two powerful and fashionable objections are raised against
this confident trust in the general reliability of the Gospel records. The first is called historical relativism. This is really a
very radical kind of historical scepticism. It believes that it is
never really possible to get back to what happened because the
accounts come to us refracted through the prism of the subjectivity of the Gospel writers. Their own historical situation,
it is held, unconsciously influences what they say, and really
tells us more about the situation in which they wrote than about
the situations they are attempting to describe. In other words,
what we have in the Gospels is what the early church *made* of
Jesus, rather than a reliable and objective historical record.
Each story grew out of the needs of the early church as it faced
its own problems, while it meditated on the memory of the
earthly Jesus. The account of the stilling of the storm, for instance, really only tells us how the early church coped with the
storms that were falling upon it. The event described by Mark
is really a parable which encouraged the first Christians to trust
in the presence of the Christ of faith in the storm-tossed boat
of the persecuted church. Attractive as this approach may be
to a certain kind of modern mind, I believe that it is really a
kind of despair. I believe that it also approaches dishonesty. On
this view, we are exhorted to find strength and consolation in

accounts that *intend* to be historical descriptions but are, in fact, only to be taken as encouraging stories. Where, then, lies the basis for the trust? Apparently, it lies not in the one who saves us but in our own subjective use of a species of fable.

Thomas Torrance has some trenchant words on this approach. He says that the problem concerns the "intention" of the Gospel writers:

> When you make a statement you intend to refer to something of which you have some experience or idea in yourself: Here you have a subjective pole, the mind of the speaker, and an objective pole, the thing referred to. According to William of Occam, we are more sure of the state of our own mind or soul than of the external referent or existent, that is, of what he called *the oblique intention* rather than *the direct intention* (which is what the statement refers to). Roughly speaking, two different views diverged from this point. What do we do when we interpret the Holy Scriptures? How do we regard the relations between the words and the things they signify? Erasmus took up Occam's doctrine of intention but gave it a more psychological and ethical turn . . . he penetrated into the subjective pole by reading what they wrote as expressions of their inner experience. Thus there began what has come to be known as 'modernism', a reinterpretation of Christianity through redacting its direct statements about God and His saving acts in our world into statements expressing inward moral states or attitudes of soul. Calvin, like Luther, took the opposite point of view in which he sought to interpret the Scriptures mainly in accordance with their direct intention, that is, by following the intention of the biblical writers through to the realities they intended their statements to refer to. They took this from Hilary of Poitiers who laid it down that we must not subordinate things to the words that indicate them, but the words to the things they indicate, for it is of the things themselves that we think rather than the words used of them (*God and Rationality*; London: Oxford University Press, 1971, p. 36).

The point is really of profound importance because it

concerns the very heart of the human predicament. Our problem is our self-centeredness, the profound difficulty we find in being liberated from our own imprisonment to ourselves. The very center of the Christian claim lies in the assertion that God has intervened in a decisive way in our affairs, that he has broken into the prison of our own selfhood and freed us. It is based upon the claim that there *is* something out there; that we are not forever bound in our own thought processes and psychological experiences. There is One outside ourselves who has broken in upon us and our world and with whom we can, even now, have a saving relationship. That *was* the good news: God has acted in Christ on our behalf. It is really a form of perversity to reverse that bracing and liberating fact, and throw everything back upon our own mental structures. It is really a form of that self-centeredness against which Jesus mounted an unremitting attack. He called us to come out of ourselves, to open ourselves, like children, to the wonder and reality of One present in our midst to save. It is tragic that much modern theology has crawled back inside the prison house and told us that there is no liberator that we can turn to, that we are still on our own, albeit with a few new stories to pass the time with. I feel certain that we must turn from this kind of subjectivism, and affirm the saving facts of the gospel as *facts* that are, in some real sense, independent of our apprehension and mode of transmission of them. The modern method of radical historical relativism reduces Jesus to a vanishing point and throws us back upon ourselves. It places us exactly alongside those who failed to open themselves to our Lord in his earthly ministry precisely because they got in their own way. What they then experienced was not the visitation of the living God but their own subjective reaction to his challenge and demand. They were, we read, offended at him.

> "Unless ye become as little children ye cannot enter the kingdom of heaven."

The fact is that behind much that is paraded as modern historiography there lie certain dominant philosophical assumptions which are allowed to influence and control the approach to the evidence offered by the New Testament writers.

Some words quoted by Bishop Gore from Bishop Creighton illuminate this very well.

> Historical criticism is not a science: it is only an investigation of the value of evidence. It rests on presuppositions which are derived from experience. I am disposed to believe what is analogous to my experience: my criticism is awakened by what is not analogous. The destructive criticism of the New Testament rests on the presupposition that miracles do not happen. As the writers of the New Testament record miracles it is necessary to explain how these records came into being. A number of ingenious and plausible theories about their nature and authorship and gradual growth have consequently been formed. Their number and persistency seem to add to their force. You say, 'Why are they not refuted?' The only possible refutation of them is to show that, apart from the presuppositions on which they rest, their conclusions are not capable of positive proof. . . . The miracles connected with the person of Jesus are analogous to the spiritual experience of the believing Christian. Therefore he is not moved by the presupposition that they are contrary to nature. The real question in dispute is the conception of nature. Biblical criticism will not solve that question (quoted in Gore, *Belief in God*, p. 229).

This brings us to the second major objection which has been brought against the New Testament record, the attack upon the authenticity of the miraculous element in the narrative. I have called it "the miraculous element," but that choice of words, though it is common, is very misleading. It creates the impression that the accounts of miracles can somehow be excised from the Gospels without destroying their coherence. This is hardly the case. If the possibility of the miraculous is rejected, it involves such major surgery upon the historical record as to leave it maimed and lacking in coherent development. On every level the account given of Christ presupposes and depends upon the existence of the supernatural and its interaction, through Christ, with the natural. Again, our use of language traps us. Words like "natural" and "supernatural"

suggest impersonal realities or energies, whereas the whole genius of biblical religion is its insistence upon the personal category when it talks about God. We are not dealing with a
category called "the supernatural," but with the living, personal
approach of our heavenly Father. Part of the difficulty here is
the way we objectify metaphors and become their prisoners.
For a very long time now, the prevalent image for describing
nature has been mechanistic. A machine is a construct which
works according to predictable laws. Applied to nature this
leads to a theory called "determinism" which holds that everything is part of a causal sequence which, if sufficient information is available, is entirely predictable. There are scientists
who apply the same theory to human nature and who claim
that there is no such thing as human freedom: everything we
do is entirely determined by factors beyond our control. Now,
it is certainly true that our freedom as individuals is drastically
modified in all sorts of ways, by all sorts of factors such as
inheritance, social and environmental context, as well as the
cumulative effect of all the past choices we have made. Nevertheless, it is a widely held assumption that we have a significant
level of control over the choices we make. Common sense,
whose intuitions are frequently close to the truth, simply af-
firms the fact, however it may go on to qualify the judgment
in particular circumstances. Human freedom, therefore, seems
to provide us with another model for interpreting reality, this
time not a mechanistic model but a personal one. It is at least
theoretically possible to believe that, if there is a god who is in
some sense personal, and if he is the creator and sustainer of
the natural universe, he will be capable of particular interven-
tions in the order of things that may appear to be contrary to
that order on one level but are in fact simply an expression of
the ultimate order, which is the divine, personal will. Our own
experience of life provides us with an analogy. The human will
is not content to operate within the narrow confines of nature.
It has "improved" nature in all sorts of ways, and even thwarted
nature by using her against herself. In other words, there has
been, since the emergence of reason in humankind, a factor
which has transcended nature. Our own personal experience
also verifies this. Our life generally runs along fairly predictable lines, but we are capable, when the occasion demands it,

of unusual and unpredictable activity for the sake of some special end. Now, it is certainly not easy to believe in miracles, but is it not at least hypothetically possible that if God is the sort of God the prophets say he is, he should be capable of special activity that appears to contradict that order of nature of which he is author and sustainer?

There is a further point that suggests itself. There is a lot of evidence which suggests that human beings in advanced or heightened states of consciousness are able to act in ways that seem to contradict what we believe to be the closed and predictable order of nature. To give only two examples: there is a great deal of evidence to attest the strange phenomenon of *fire-walking* and endurance of other usually injurious practices; and *levitation* is a phenomenon which is attested throughout history. There is considerable evidence, too, that many of these phenomena have been repudiated by the scientific establishment on what appear to be doctrinal grounds rather than on a proper investigation of the evidence—another example of the powerful effect prejudice can have upon one's apprehension of objective fact. In his book *Natural and Supernatural*, Brian Inglis has recently documented what appears to be a major scientific cover-up of supernatural phenomena. I am not in any way able to assess the particular merit of all his findings, but their cumulative effect is very impressive. If human beings are capable of such baffling violations of the apparently stable order of nature in response to some higher imperative, why should not God be thought capable of such creative innovations as accord with his purpose for the world? The fact is, however, that though, from our perspective, these innovative initiatives of God appear to be breaches of law, they are in fact congruent with the deepest moral order and purpose of the world. This is the point Augustine makes in certain frequently quoted words on the subject:

> Not unreasonably we say that God does something contrary to nature which he does contrary to what we know in nature. For this is what we call nature—the customary course of nature as known to us, against which, when God does anything, they are called marvels or miracles. But as to that supreme law of nature, which is hidden

from our knowledge either because we are impious or because we are still deficient in power to understand, God can no more act contrary to it than he can act contrary to himself (*Contra Faustum* XXVI.3).

If I may be allowed for the moment to ignore the foundational miracles of the Christian religion, namely the Incarnation and the Resurrection, we can say that Christ's miracles have a double purpose in the divine strategy. First of all, they are *significant*, that is to say, they point beyond themselves to a deeper meaning. In John's Gospel the miracles he records are called "signs." The old, simple definition was "a wonder with a meaning in it." Each event is a marvel, something unusual, which the experienced order is unable to account for. It is a sign which calls men to an act of recognition and interpretation: here is a special work of God; here is an event which signals, to those who read it aright, that God is not absent from the created order. They are inbreakings of God's special rule into the apparently iron rule of nature. They are in fact, in modern jargon, revolutionary gestures, signs of resistance to an overweening power. This is closely related to the second purpose of Christ's miracles: they are *restorative* or *renovative*. These are both terms which are applied to the remaking of old buildings. That is the kind of force the words have in this context too. God's created universe has fallen into decay: the miracles are acts of restoration which point to the original plan and intention of the builder. They are also, in some sense, signs to us of what nature in full and free relationship with God is capable of. From this point of view the miracles of Christ are natural—the natural outflowings of the power which he possessed by virtue of his relationship with God. His miracles can be seen, therefore, as pledges of what a restored humanity would be capable of.

I have labored this because I wanted to try to show you that much of the attack upon the trustworthiness of the New Testament is not due to marvelous new historical discoveries which put the whole thing in a new light. Most of the current criticisms of the historical integrity of the New Testament have been around a long time and are really based on certain assumptions that are brought to the evidence and allowed to tamper with it. In weighing any kind of evidence we are dealing in probabilities, not in attainable certainties. All that I want to achieve is the acceptance of the position that it is perfectly honest to find in the New Testament a broad trustworthiness, provided one does not bring to it certain massive assumptions that advance a veto against its central claim before looking at the evidence for it. Ever since the philosopher David Hume, Western intellectuals have held that the presumption of truth was always against miracles and that it was safe to assume as a working hypothesis that they never occurred. That is a clear and water-tight position. So water-tight, in fact, that it can protect you absolutely from any overture that God might make to you in history, because such an overture must, in the nature of the case, be a break in the system of the universe as we understand it. For a mind so protected against revelation's inrush it is certainly true that "if they hear not Moses and the prophets, they will not believe though one were to rise from the dead." But what if one did rise from the dead? What if God has "visited his people"? What if the Word *was* made flesh? It would be eternally sad to miss such a momentous appointment on the grounds that it couldn't logically happen. What if it did?

PART TWO

The Wisdom of God

CHAPTER FIVE

The Riddle of Jesus

I ended the last chapter with a question, and it was not meant to be rhetorical. I asked, in effect, what if God has taken a mysterious initiative and entered the historical process the better to be known by his children? In the nature of the case a claim like that cannot be put to an absolutely logical test. This accounts for the frustration that certain kinds of philosophers feel when they study the Christian claim. We usually try to make sense of things we don't understand by some sort of translation into things we do. If you come across a word you don't know, you find out its meaning by looking it up in a dictionary which expresses its meaning in words you *do* know. All this sort of activity presupposes the continuity of experience: we operate on the logic of precedence. We gain a hold on what is unfamiliar by means of the familiar, by a process of accumulation. This epistemological conservatism always makes the task of new knowledge extremely difficult, and history is full of examples of the resistance of cultural, scientific, and intellectual establishments to the intrusion of new knowledge. (I have, for instance, just read a fascinating account of the opposition of the American medical establishment in the 19th century to Dr. Oliver Wendell Holmes' claim that most cases of puerperal fever were actually transmitted by doctors who paid no attention to the need to disinfect themselves when they had been in touch with a case of the fever. They themselves were the main carriers of the contagion that killed so many women in childbirth, but they refused to accept the evidence that was offered because they were in thrall to another theory.)

If this inertia operates against new knowledge on the *natural* level, it will be immediately obvious that it will raise almost insuperable objections against claims that can only be described as *supernatural*. By definition, such claims cannot be verified on the natural level. It is true, of course, that many scholars have offered naturalistic explanations of the supernatural claim, but then they only succeed in explaining it away; they effectively remove the distinctive element in the claim. The claim, to put it simply, is that there has been an intrusion of the divine into the natural sphere. In the words of the song of Zacharias, "God has visited his people." If you take the events that are claimed to embody that visitation and explain them naturalistically, you have, in fact, dismissed the claim totally: "Is not this *Joseph's* son?" On one level, this is all too easily done. The revelatory events were, after all, events, happenings in time. People came to these events freighted with all sorts of prejudices and presuppositions. The most natural thing to do was to interpret everything that happened and every claim that was made *according to precedent*. That is always the way we work and it is, in fact, the wisest way the world knows. History is full of frauds and madmen and extraordinary claims. Hume's tough-minded scepticism is the best approach in most circumstances. Unless, of course, God has acted in a quite new and special way! If that has happened, then the accumulated wisdom of centuries is unable to respond to the divine overture. It has made itself blind and deaf and incapable of receiving the revelation, precisely because it has settled the whole question in advance. This fundamental scepticism has become the prevailing mindset of our era. Even within the Christian theological tradition in the West it reigns supreme. It is the invisible but powerful assumption behind much of the New Testament criticism of our time. Those who are governed by it but who wish to remain within the Christian tradition go to extraordinary lengths to maintain some sort of intellectual integrity as they continue to use the language of faith. The most popular device is to lump almost all the language of Christian theology within the category of "myth." This is an elusive term which has almost as many meanings as it has defenders, but much of it boils down to a simple translation technique. You take all the embarrassing language about divine initiative and action and you translate it into this-worldly categories. You find a natural meaning that people can lay hold of and you translate the offending claim into it without remainder. The Resurrection of Jesus Christ from the dead, for instance, is translated into an experience within the disciples by which they became persuaded that the spirit and standards of Jesus lived on and were worth dying for. The technique is commonplace and need not be elaborated any further here. It is a simple, brilliant, and, for many, liberating way of retaining the old categories without actually having to be embarrassed by them.

Now, it is obviously very important to many people to be able to do this, and I'm not sure that I want to oppose them for it. F. D. Maurice said that men were usually right in what they affirmed and wrong in what they denied. Maybe we should be content that many men and women who have difficulties with the Christian tradition have found this way of staying within it. Maybe we should be content to let them affirm what they can and leave it at that. *They* don't, of course. Many of the proponents of this school are quite aggressively certain that this is the *only* way to handle the tradition and that those of us who give the ancient language more substantial meaning are, quite simply, wrong. So it is not just a matter of gentle theological tolerance. Something is being contended for. For my part, I am content to allow people to use the category of myth in this way, though I am quite persuaded that its appeal is limited to a certain type of intellectual and that it limits the power that the Christian claim might have to change the hearts and minds of men and women. For what are we left with? The thing that men and women long to know and believe, if only they can learn how, is that God has visited and redeemed them, that he has come toward them in a quite definite and distinctive and unique way. Learning how to respond to that divine overture is, of course, our great problem, but it is surely no solution to the problem to be told that we don't, in fact, have to wrestle with it *because nothing new has happened*. We are still back where we were with all our old experiences of life and nature and history. The new thing isn't new at all. The break in the wall, the tear in the curtain, is not real: it is only a way of talking about where we've always been. We are still locked into our Godfast system of nature and its predictable pattern. We are still imprisoned by the sullen determinism of history. But what if God has broken into our prison and come among us? By definition all our precedents won't help us, because God's action would be unprecedented. None of our old experiences will help us because this would be a radically new experience. In the face of this approach by God we are left either absolutely naked or so heavily armed and blinkered that we are impervious to his overtures. As I read the New Testament I see an enormous struggle going on between these two responses. Paul tells us that it is the world's very wisdom which places it in the gravest danger because that wisdom has no category by which it can interpret the scandalous overture of God. The paradox is that it was the foolish, the poor, the childlike, who somehow found the freshness, the openness to recognize the One who had come, while everyone else busily tried to interpret him away: "Is not this Joseph's son?"

So we come up against something hard and almost impossibly difficult: we have to unlearn our wisdom and sophistication if we would see God in Christ; we have to be stripped of all that we are in order to be clothed with the new garments that God would have us wear. And Hume can't help us here! Our speech and all its ancient cleverness has somehow to cease if God's Word would be heard, and then God has to teach us a whole new grammar. Is not this what confronts us on page after page of the New Testament? We can feel the strain placed upon the disciples as every category they trusted in was stripped from them, reversed, turned upside down. We can feel the emotion of Jesus as he tries to break through the armor plate over their hearts and minds. The revelation of God in Christ had to burn through all the accumulated defenses of history in order to find an answer from the human heart. And it still has to. It has to penetrate mountains of argument and cross oceans of language in order to utter a single Word. It's as though God were all the time trying to speak to us and we could not hear him above the din of our own liturgy. Is it not time for us to be silent so that we might listen? If God has spoken and acted, or if it is claimed that he has, surely we must stop everything else and go and see what has come to pass, exactly like the shepherds in the fields above Bethlehem. And remember, we've got to leave all our weapons outside the door.

We've got to cast aside every assumption that would seek an advantage from God, every presupposition that would limit him, every preference that would twist him to our own purpose. We are going to take the risk of letting God speak what is in his heart. Our tendency will be to put our own case. We won't really listen to him because while he speaks we'll be preparing our own response. It took the shock of the Crucifixion and the silencing wonder of the Resurrection to get the disciples to pay attention, and at last they did. We have to do the same, and it is even more difficult for us because we have an added problem. The revelation came direct to them. It comes to us in some sense refracted through the evangelists, and our old enemy will take every opportunity to fasten on *them* and not on *Him*. But we have a friend as well. I have already said that when the Word is preached there are two that bear witness: there is the Word that is spoken and there is the Spirit of God within us which goes out in response to it. God is working on our side, too. We can learn to answer from within if only we'll humble and silence ourselves and let the Spirit guide us to him who is Truth.

> Soul, self; come, poor Jackself, I do advise
> You, jaded, let be; call off thoughts awhile
> Elsewhere; leave comfort root-room; let joy size
> At God knows when to God knows what; whose smile
> 's not wrung, see you; unforeseen times rather—as
>   skies
> Betweenpie mountains—lights a lovely mile
> (G. M. Hopkins, "My Own Heart").

The Christian claim was put with refreshing brevity by St. Paul: "God was in Christ reconciling the world to himself." A little later it was put with equal brevity by St. John: "The Word was made flesh and dwelt among us." Of course the phrase "God was in Christ" and the highly concentrated term "the Word" are packed with meaning, but the meaning is clear. In the words of the Athanasian Creed:

> We believe and confess that our Lord Jesus Christ, the Son of God, is both God and Man. He is God, of the

Substance of the Father, begotten before the worlds: and
he is Man, of the Substance of his Mother, born in the
world.

Now before our minds start picking holes in the words, let us
be quite sure of the experience which the words inadequately
convey. And here I have to fall back again on the other witness
to these matters: the inward testimony of the Holy Spirit. The
words themselves can never convey the experience. All they
do is stretch language to the breaking point by seeking to contain within the limits of expression that which is illimitable and
inexpressible. This is the ancient frustration of the poet seeking to describe a wild northern sunset to a company of the
blind. He knows what he sees and he longs for us to see it
through his own eyes: instead we *hear* it through his *words* and
fail utterly to have the experience. It is the old problem of
intention again. The evangelist is wildly beseeching us to look
toward *Jesus*, but we remain fixated upon his own strange behavior and extraordinary language. The words, of themselves,
are *nothing*, were never meant to be anything. What the speak-
ers want us to do is to stand where they stand and look where
they look and gaze upon him whom they gaze upon. When
and if we can get ourselves into that position, we find that we
are looking toward Jesus and away from ourselves and even
away from the evangelists, and we find the response rising
within us, we recognize him as they recognized him. And what
we see is God's face turned toward us in love and torment.
That is what we mean by Revelation and Incarnation: in Jesus
Christ God's heart became visible to us. The evangelists' experience of Jesus was an experience of God, not obliquely or
by some process of indirection, but directly and absolutely. And
they didn't *think* their way to this recognition: it was shocked
out of them, it *hit* them: "My Lord and my God." Jesus Christ
henceforth was their absolute, their Lord, the very identity of
God himself. Language was never able to capture or keep up
with that primary shock of recognition.

The intoxicated and untidy poetry of the New Testament
was followed later by the more precise terminology of the
creeds, but the Fathers never claimed that they had finally
caught the lark in their cage. That was never the purpose of

the formulae they adopted. The real purpose of the creeds was negative. In Athanasius' phrase, "the creeds were signposts against heresy"; they warned people away from the danger zones of over-precision because they soon recognized that the attempt to capture the wild and aweful reality of the experience of Christ in a neat proposition always ended in a radical limiting of what they knew the truth to be. The experience was too wide and overwhelming ever to be captured in words. The great heretics, however, were like temperance reformers who wanted to control and rationalize this wild and extravagant claim. They always wanted to tame and limit the paradoxical fullness of revelation by cutting it and drying it, by boxing and confining it. They had a fatal passion for neatness. They wanted all the wildness and untidiness stamped out. A good heresy is always a neat thing, purged of all paradox and wildness. We tend to think that heretics are daring and adventurous men, held back by the timid conformity of the narrowly orthodox. That is just about as complete a reversal of fact as you can get. It is precisely the width and excitement of orthodoxy that offends the narrow unimaginativeness of the heretic. He wants a manageable and symmetrical doctrine to preach: not for him the violent paradoxes and contradictions of the tradition. He wants something that will go down easily, so he knocks off the jagged edges, the abrasive little contours that tend to catch in the throat of the world. And they all end by making the experience smaller than it was. They capture an aspect and call it the whole. They cut the gospel down to their own size. A heresy is never a liberating thing. It's the opposite. It wants to shut the gates, not leave them open. It is always a limiting of the illimitable. It is the heretics who try to capture the lark in their cages. The Catholic Church has never claimed to be able to do such a thing: like a mad Russian novelist she has always told her children they must learn to have it both ways. They must live with the tensions and antinomies of the experience of Christ. They are proclaiming an experience that was never translatable into adequate language, anyway. Let them, therefore, celebrate the contradictions, but never attempt to resolve them. The language of the creeds is closer to poetry than to geometry: it wants us to listen to the lark sing, not try to trap him. Bishop John Robinson wrote a book some years ago which

I never got around to reading; it was called *But That I Can't Believe*. I'm sure it was impeccably orthodox; nevertheless its title could serve as a motto for the heretical mind which is always announcing its difficulty with this or that, always telling us what it *can't* believe. People of this sort always end up by getting us to look at *them* and their ideas and what they can or cannot stomach. The point of concentration is always upon what *they* make of the revelation and only in a very secondary sense upon the revelation itself. Speaking personally, I have long since grown weary of this. I am not any longer interested in human opinions on this life-or-death matter because I know they cannot save me. Professor Brown's ideas may be clever and fascinating, but I am a drowning man and need something he cannot offer. With Paul I know that no human gospel will answer the problem posed by the human condition. Only the Word of God will do. Only God can pluck my feet out of the net of human opinions that trap me. Has that Word been uttered, then? Has God so acted? Yes, says the apostolic church. Look toward Jesus and away from yourselves and you will find God in your midst: Jesus Emmanuel, God with us.

But how did they come to that amazing recognition? Nowadays as we look at the record of the revelation, we see it, as it were, through the wrong end of the telescope. We have to beat back upstream to the source. We are not offered the chronological neatness of conventional biography. When we first discover the followers of Christ after his death, they are busily proclaiming that he is alive! Paul's preaching invited people to share in a present experience of a living Jesus. He did not ask them to participate in a bout of historical reminiscence. Nevertheless, we can be fairly certain from what we know of the formation of the Gospel record that the early church went back again and again to their memories of the earthly Jesus and interpreted their experience of him in the light of what they had now come to believe about him. And what emerges is a drama of revelation's struggle with the ignorance and slowness of its chosen witnesses. The picture is of a piece with what William Temple called the progressive revelation of God to the Old Testament prophets, except that what was then bits and pieces now focusses into a clear picture of a God wrestling with the hearts and minds of those with whom he would communicate. Like us, the chosen witnesses kept getting themselves in the way of God's showing of himself. They were loaded with preconceptions and misconceptions, and they kept trying to edit the terrifying reality of God into something acceptable to themselves. They wanted to conventionalize God's approach. They were incapable of letting God be God. It is to their eternal credit that they seem to have made little attempt to touch up the picture so that it would be more flattering to themselves.

If you look through the eyes of the evangelists toward Jesus and not at the evangelists themselves, a certain freshness of vision occurs, a sense of excitement and surprise begins to grow. Instead of focussing on the evangelists and asking ourselves, "If this is what they felt moved to write about him, what can we discover about Jesus from an analysis of the process they went through in compiling the record?", we must try to imitate Hilary of Poitiers' important canon of interpretation— namely, that we must not subordinate things to the words that indicate them, but the words to the things they indicate, for it is of the things themselves that we must think rather than the words used of them. What we have to submit to is an act of intellectual conversion whereby we learn to look through the record to the one it points to. We must, in the words of the Letter to the Hebrews, "look toward Jesus." Of course there are all sorts of technical issues surrounding the record and there is a time and a place for paying attention to them, but not now. When you are drowning you don't waste time on a minute inspection of the life jacket that is thrown to you—you grab it desperately. The revelation of God in Jesus Christ is God's last throw toward us. Let us try to lay hold of it.

As we look, then, at Jesus through the eyes of the evangelists, one of the first things that strikes us is the mystery surrounding him. We confront a personality which towers over history and still flames out toward us. It would be quite wrong to talk about the *attractiveness* of Jesus, though there are touches of humor and tenderness in the picture that are captivating. What comes through, above all, is a sense of awe that contains elements of terror and fear, as well as fascination. The sentimentality of generations has tamed Jesus into a kind of vicarage pussycat, but C. S. Lewis was surely right to liken him to a lion.

But no zoological analogy can come at all close to the reality of that overwhelming presence which combined fierce tenderness with angry love. He is one with the God of the prophets who roared from Zion, yet wept over his children. There is something scalding about this Jesus, something that consumes like fire. Whence came he? That is the mystery his hearers sought to answer. He was an enigma.

> "Where did this man get all this? What is the wisdom given to him? What mighty works are wrought by his hands! Is not this the carpenter, the son of Mary and brother of James and Joses and Judas and Simon, and are not his sisters here with us?" And they took offense at him (Mark 6:2-3).

The choice of words is highly significant. ·It was contrary to Jewish usage to describe a man as the son of his mother, even when she was a widow, except when you wanted to insult him. Rumors circulated in his own lifetime that Jesus was illegitimate. John records an encounter with the Jews in which they said to him: "*We* were not born of fornication; we have one Father, even God." John was well aware of the irony in that claim. He had taken the mother of Jesus into his own home, and he must have been well aware of the circumstance of his birth. Several commentators, notably Hoskyns and Temple, see an allusion to the birth of Jesus in what John says in verse 13 of his Gospel when he is describing those who receive the Word of God and believe in his name: "who were born, not of blood nor of the will of the flesh nor of the will of man, but of God." There is, however, no explicit reference in John to the Virgin Birth. What we are given is the birth of Christ seen from the perspective of eternity, from the very heart of God. His birth, according to John, was not the result of a random act of sexual intercourse. It was the result of a determinate act of God. The Word who had existed with God before time, took flesh in time, "for us men and our salvation." John makes the claim quite explicit: Jesus Christ had his origin in God, he came from God. Matthew and Luke make the same claim in a less theological, more historical way. They state that the birth of Jesus was caused by the direct intervention of God and not by any

man. Jesus was not the son of Joseph, nor was he the illegitimate son of an unknown father, as rumor had it: he was born
of Mary by the Holy Spirit. His origin lay, not in the will of
man but in the direct initiative of God. This, of course, is a
notorious problem for some modern theologians, who have
gone to extraordinary lengths to get around the acute embarrassment of it all. They have recourse to various devices. The
evangelists, they say, are making a theological statement, not a
historical one, and the story is not to be taken literally. Luke's
own opening paragraph does not offer any support to that
conclusion:

> Inasmuch as many have undertaken to compile a narra-
> tive of the things which have been accomplished among
> us, just as they were delivered to us by those who from
> the beginning were eyewitnesses and ministers of the
> word, it seemed good to me also, having followed all
> things closely for some time past, to write an orderly ac-
> count for you, most excellent Theophilus, that you may
> know the truth concerning the things of which you have
> been informed (Luke 1:1-4).

Luke claims to be giving us history, and there is nothing in
Matthew that leads us to suppose that that was not also his
intention.

Another device is the suggestion that Matthew and Luke
were trying to obtain supernatural credit for Jesus by conform-
ing his birth to the legends that surrounded the birth of various
semi-divine heroes in the Hellenistic pantheon. Numerous
scholars have pointed out that all the precedents are of gods
having sexual intercourse with humans and never of a *virgin*
birth, but the very suggestion itself is insulting to the integrity
of the Christian tradition. It belongs to an approach which
accounts for the supernatural element in the Gospels by claiming that it got there from the mystery religions and pagan
myths. It is, of course, impossible either to verify or falsify this
claim, which accounts for its tenacity in certain quarters. I have
never had explained to me how these external influences upon
the primitive record worked. Were Matthew and Luke in some
sense hypnotized by a pervasive psychic contagion which led

them, separately, either to create or give credence to totally erroneous claims? Or did they just make them up and then soberly set them forth as history?

The same subtle kind of character assassination lies behind the suggestion that Matthew in particular industriously created fictitious events in our Lord's life in order to square them with Old Testament prophecy. Others gratefully pounce upon the differences in the accounts of our Lord's birth found in Matthew and Luke. Differences there are, but most of them can be accounted for by the obvious deduction that Luke writes from the perspective of Mary, and Matthew from that of Joseph. In all essential details they are in agreement.

Behind all these attempts to explain away the accounts of the Virgin Birth there lies the same assumption we have already discussed: miracles of this sort cannot happen. Certainly, there is no precedent in history for a virgin birth. Nor is there any precedent for the Incarnation of God in the person of Jesus Christ. The central offense of the Christian claim lies here: that we are confronted with a wholly new act of God, a new "let there be," and none of our human categories will help us interpret it. We have to discover within ourselves the ability to call off thought awhile elsewhere and let God speak to us a new word which is discontinuous with all our previous experience. It is this new creation which we are called to share in, but we cannot partake in it if we bind ourselves so absolutely to the old.

At the end we are left with a simple historical dilemma. The rumors about the illegitimacy of Jesus attest to the fact that Joseph was not his father. How was he conceived, then? The New Testament writers do not give us their sources, but we can safely conclude that the account came from the family of Jesus, almost certainly from Mary herself. They claim that he was born of the virgin Mary by the Holy Spirit. It is almost impossible to account for the story if it is not true, unless we are prepared to state quite bluntly that Jesus was a bastard and that the early church lied about his origins. When you remove all the scholarly subtlety that surrounds the debate, that is what it comes down to. The followers of him who was the truth fabricated an extraordinary story, which was intrinsically unbelievable, in order to cover up the sad truth. Strictly speaking, there is a profound and poetic irony in this ancient slander that is cast upon the origins of Jesus: God made himself fatherless for love of children who had orphaned themselves. In a real sense Jesus had no earthly legitimacy, he was never to be conformed to the standard of the world. From the manger on, he was always to be a sign of contradiction and offense.

If the self-disclosure of God in Jesus Christ is the main theme of the New Testament record, the second theme must surely be the drama of the gradual recognition by his closest followers of who he was; and related to this is the wave of hostility and rejection by his fellow-countrymen which finally brought him to death on a cross. Whatever motive we attribute to those who executed him (and the conviction of Jesus seems to have been that it was due as much to tragic ignorance as to culpable wickedness), the final impression one gains from the New Testament is that his death was not a simple event isolated by its historical context and limited and defined by its immediate causality. (One of the hideous consequences of this limited view has been the hounding of the Jews by generations of Christians, although this ugly and continuing reaction is also part of the external meaning of that one death: God is put to a *perpetual* shame.) John's Gospel is the most profound meditation in the tradition upon the total meaning of Jesus, and he tells us that "No one has ever seen God; the only Son, who is in the bosom of the Father, he has made him known." What is revealed in time in the life and death of Jesus is the heart of the Father and the way he deals with the ancient tragedy of his estranged creation. The life of Jesus was a revelation in time of an endless truth about God's way with us. It was a "miniaturization" of an enormous reality, reduced in scale so that we might at last understand it. Helen Waddell puts the truth of it into the mouth of Abelard's friend Thibault:

> He pointed to a fallen tree beside them sawn through the middle. "That dark ring there, it goes up and down the whole length of the tree. But you only see it where it is cut across. That is what Christ's life was; the bit of God that we saw. And we think God is like that, because Christ was like that, kind, and forgiving sins and healing people.

We think God is like that for ever, because it happened
once, with Christ. But not the pain. Not the agony at the
last. We think that stopped."

We, too, think that stopped, because the reality is too awful for
us to bear. As Abelard whispered in response,

" . . . you think that all the pain of the world was Christ's
cross?"

"God's cross," said Thibault. "And it goes on" (Peter
Abelard; London: Constable and Company, 1933, p. 290).

This is why Christians endlessly meditate upon the life and
death of Jesus in liturgy and private devotion and personal
study. They have, under the gentle prompting of the Spirit of
Jesus who guides them, learned that the New Testament record
is an opening into the heart of God. It shows us God's way with
us now. In the next chapter I shall spend some time looking
at the very center of that burning focus of revelation, the death
of Christ. Meanwhile I want to return to the life and work of
Christ, for that too was part of the showing forth of the eternal
heart of God.

In the prophets we catch flaming glimpses of the reality
of God's suffering love, as he wrestles with us and with his own
mysterious nature. The prophets, too, provide us with a genuine, if partial, disclosure of God. We discover there an extraordinary tension, an ambivalence in the divine nature. (I am
well aware of the dangers of such language, but how else is one
to talk about such mysteries?) What was hinted at in riddle and
poem in the prophets becomes explicit, is placarded in large
letters in the ministry of Christ. Part of this process of expli-
cation involved the training of the disciples to *see* who was
acting in their midst so that they might, at last, understand the
meaning of what was done. "Have you not yet understood?"
is the poignant question which punctuates the narrative. What
they saw at first was a baffling yet compelling puzzle. They
were called to a companionship that promised every fulfilment
of human longing, yet they translated this immediately into
terms they understood: power and status. They even quarreled
among themselves as to which would be greatest in the society

that was promised. They were captivated by the mercy and tenderness of Jesus, yet they wanted to keep it for themselves. They tried to hold back the needy and the children from Christ, to shove back all the imploring hands that were thrust at him wherever he went. And they were dismayed and angered by his strange changes of mood, by the sudden rushes of vehemence and denunciation. They were enchanted by his tenderness and appalled by his stringency: "Who then can be saved?" It is exactly our response. We snip from the records of the disclosure what is of comfort and support, and shrink from or interpret away what offends or frightens us. The truth is that there is as much fear as comfort in the New Testament, for there is anger as well as mercy in God. God is offended by our slowness and laziness, our moral and spiritual idleness. His anger is always at the boiling point with us, and in constant tension with his love for us, that engulfing tenderness that also floods the pages of the Old Testament. His anger competes with his love. His justice wrestles with his mercy. Ambition for what we might become struggles with acceptance of what we are.

And this conflict in God seems to correspond with our experience of our own nature. Do we not spend our lives caught somewhere between self-loathing and self-satisfaction? Is not our longing for holiness and goodness constantly modified by a strange and persistent moral inertia, our desire for life made forfeit by a constant impulse toward self-destruction? God's ambivalence toward us seems exactly mirrored in the radical ambivalence we experience in our own nature. Indeed, these two seem but different aspects of the one reality, and that reality speaks of division, of a great rent that has torn through time and its children. Which of us in our reaction to the sins of others does not halt frequently between condemnation and tenderness? Our ambition for their glorification and holiness is made weak and feeble by a terrible tenderness for them, a complete acceptance of them as they are. As condemnation rises in us, so do the words of Psalm 103:

> God knoweth whereof we are made: he remembereth that we are but dust.

Who can expect much of dust?

This dazzling ambiguity is seen in Jesus, the Jesus who is the mystery who makes of the two, one. Decent, liberal-minded Western Christians have projected so much of themselves onto Jesus that they no longer confront him in his scandalous reality. Jesus, in fact, was a spiritual terrorist. In Jesus man's moral failure is taken with absolute seriousness. You sense in him a terrible urgency to call men to account, by reason of the great danger they are in. He calls them to repent, to turn back before it is too late. The mystery of retribution in the message of Jesus is as unavoidable as it is unfashionable. It lashes out at us from the pages of the Gospels and it has built fear and offense into Christian history. Fear, because which of us does not stand justly condemned? And offense, because which of us does not know in his heart that he is sin's victim as well as its agent? So the terrible judgments of Christ and his most withering denunciations are immediately succeeded by, indeed are often co-active with, a gentleness and a heartbroken pity for us in our lostness. You sense the overwhelming force of his desire to gather us into his arms as a hen gathers her brood under her wings, and we would not. Within Jesus we find both judge and mother. We are both repelled by him and inexorably drawn toward him. To meditate on the blazing paradox of his appeal is to experience a kind of Chinese torture in which we are alternately terrified and consoled. In Jesus, somehow, we come close to total loss and total gain. We feel ourselves to be at the same time both totally rejected and utterly accepted.

The only honest way to confront the record of Jesus' life and ministry is to identify with *everyone* with whom he had to do. It is too easy to develop a comforting conspiracy theory of his rejection and death. We identify the enemies of Christ and draw in our breath at their obtuseness, while we place ourselves with his friends and followers, or at least with the humble and penitent. I have come to believe that this is a profound mistake which limits the scale of the work of Christ. It is too easy to build from it a simple morality tale. The truth is much more profound. Each of us is in some part both enemy and friend of Christ, both pharisee and heartbroken sinner. It is the terrifying inevitability of it all that must capture us. *We* are the hypocrites he excoriated, as well as the woman taken in adultery whom he absolved. *We* are the ones who betrayed him, as well as the women who followed him helplessly to the foot of the cross. The battle that raged between recognition and rejection, between good and evil, is not outside us; it is very much within us. Every twist in the drama is well represented in some facet of our life. And the final outcome is still rejection. He came to his own people, and his own people received him not. The history of Jesus Christ is a showing in time of God's way with us forever, and it is a revelation of defeat. At the end, Jesus was defeated not only by the open hostility and hatred of the establishment and the bloodlust of the mob, but by the failure and cowardice of his friends. The defeat of Jesus is the final demonstration of the incapacity of man to know and follow God. The split in his nature is something he cannot himself heal. He is divided against himself so that he cannot even do the things that he would. He is at war with himself and is never able to bring peace to himself. He has stoned the prophets because their words only pronounce a judgment he has already pronounced upon himself. Who can bear to hear another echo his own deep knowledge of his own baseness? Now he turns against God himself: "Here is the son; let us destroy him."

What we have to try to do, therefore, is to see what was happening from God's side. It is too obvious and predictable from the human side, this story of an incarnate goodness which goaded the self-loathing of man to murder. We have seen it too often in history and in our own experience to be surprised by it. We know enough about the defeat of good to need no reminders. What is new in this instalment of that ancient saga is that God was in it; he himself was defeated. What was he doing? What did he want us to understand? What is the death of Christ all about?

CHAPTER SIX

The Suffering God

The strangest experience of my life happened on my last day in Ghana, in March 1958. I was to sail for Britain from the port of Takoradi, and I arrived there at noon to supervise the stowing of my baggage aboard the cargo ship that was taking me home. The ship was due to sail at six in the evening, and my best friend told me he would get to the ship by the middle of the afternoon in order to see me off. I had nothing to do, so I just wandered around the docks—always a fascinating thing to do. At some point in my wandering I was approached by a tough-looking English sailor. When he heard that I had a bit of time to kill, he asked me if I'd like to come out by motorboat to his ship, which was lying far out in the harbor. I told him that I only had an hour to spare, but he assured me he'd bring me back almost immediately. It was a scruffy-looking ship and seemed to be almost completely deserted, though my new friend took me into a cabin where a few men were playing cards and drinking warm West African beer. After a quick tour of inspection I asked to be taken back, since it was nearly three o'clock and my friend might be waiting for me. By this time, anyway, I was feeling slightly uneasy. My uneasiness deepened when I was told there was no way I could get back to the dockside that night. My protests had no effect. I was a prisoner. My ship to Britain was due to sail in three hours; my friend from Accra would be wondering what had happened to me; and here was I, stuck on a strange vessel, among a group of men whose intentions baffled me. I spent three of the worst hours of my life on that ship, anchored at the entrance to the harbor. I felt completely alone and friend-less among a group of men who were mysteriously hostile to me. Soon, irrational anxieties crept in. I had visions of my ship steaming past me with my luggage on board, while I was im-prisoned aboard a ship whose name I did not know, among a group of men who filled me with a sense of horror. For the first time in my life I came close to understanding that sense of terror and anxiety that skilled practitioners of psychological torture seek to create in their victims. It is the sense of being utterly abandoned in an absolutely hostile universe. One is filled with acute anxiety and distrust. The world is a friendless place. One is not valued or loved or kept safe. One ceases to be a person and becomes a victim. Terrors and anxieties like that licked around me that afternoon. Finally, they took me back to the dockside fifteen minutes before my ship sailed. My friend was there—he had waited, with the lovely patience of the African, for three hours—but I only had time to embrace him before going on board.

Only once since then have I experienced a similar level of anxiety. I was taken to the hospital in the middle of the night. Arriving anywhere at two o'clock in the morning is a disorienting experience, and it's even worse when you're being wheeled along miles of corridor on a litter. By the time I was left to myself it was after 3 a.m. The man in the bed next to me muttered in his troubled sleep. Twenty floors below, I could hear the endless rumble of traffic on the avenue. Sud-denly, I was hit by a wave of anxiety. I was four thousand miles from home. I'd never been in a hospital before. I didn't know what was wrong with me, but I had heard the young doctor who had admitted me tell the priest who brought me in some-thing about an acute condition. The symptoms of anxiety were the same as before, but an overwhelming loneliness predomi-nated. I realized then what facing death must be like. It must be, above all, an enormous loneliness. One must face it abso-lutely alone. Loneliness. And fear, the fear that is bred of help-lessness and uncertainty.

Now, I have been fortunate in my life. I have always been surrounded by love. I am a fairly confident person. I have only rarely felt helpless and afraid. But on those two occasions I was licked by terror Not overwhelmed or swallowed up or completely undone by it, but licked, lightly touched by it. I felt its breath upon me, and it was horrifying enough. As I say, I have been fortunate, but I've known many who weren't, and I want to spend some time thinking about them, thinking about the ugly manifestations of terror and despair that afflict so many of God's children. And I have a particular reason for inviting you to take part in such a harrowing exercise. Christians spend a lot of time thinking about the death of Jesus. When we do that we are attempting two things. First of all, in some small way we are trying to enter the experience of the passion; secondly, we are trying to understand the meaning of the passion.

For Christians the death of Christ has universal implications. It was no ordinary death, it was the death of God. It was the death of God, but it was not a single dying. Rather, it was the revelation, the showing to us of a permanent reality. In a mysterious but real sense, Christ is crucified until the end of time. He partakes of all suffering in all places at all times, and that suffering has two modes: the psychological and the physical. So the death of Christ not only partakes of all suffering: it represents all suffering and evil. Christ bears it all. He bears all grief and sorrow and every pain that has ever gripped any of his children. All the ancient sorrow of humanity is portrayed in the spectacle of Christ's lonely passion. So we are called to do two difficult things: we are called to enter into his passion, but we are also called to enter into the pains and sorrow of all his children, because they are part of his cross, they are part of the story that is not yet at an end. The cross runs right through time and into eternity. When Mother Teresa cradles the emaciated body of an Indian untouchable in her arms, it is Christ she holds. When some gang of secret police drags someone from his bed in the middle of the night and takes him to a torture chamber for interrogation, it is Christ they terrify. So as we contemplate and seek, in some way, to enter the experience of Christ's passion, we are at the same time entering into the world's sorrow. But be careful. We do not do this in order to achieve an emotional catharsis, to weep satisfyingly over a picture. On the contrary, we are doing it in order to bear some of the vast burden of sorrow that lies upon human history and well-nigh crushes the joy and the meaning out of it. We try to bear some of that intolerable burden—and don't think we can't.

The human spirit is not a hermetically sealed entity. There is a mysterious rule of interchange, a marvelous chemistry of what Charles Williams called "mutual coinherence." In some sense we all dwell in each other. If we'll allow it to happen, we can set up a spiritual exchange with each other. We *can* bear another's burden, enter completely into the experience of another's sorrow, and, by so doing, somehow help to redeem it, transform it, transfigure it. I don't say remove it. We can't often do that, for reasons that do not yet appear. We can, however, help to do something much more wonderful. We can help to transmute suffering into love. Here we are at the very heart of the mystery of the gospel. I do not know if God could have banished suffering and sorrow from his universe. I do know that he has shown us that the end of all things is love, and that everything can be made to work toward that end, even the most harrowing sorrow. By bearing evil, by enduring suffering, God somehow turned these fierce enemies into friends, he transmuted all that baseness into gold: he brought forth love from the most absolute desolation. A mysterious verse from Psalm 84 always reverberates in my mind: "Who, going through the vale of misery, use it for a well, and the pools are filled with water." He uses misery as a well! He turns death into life! Nothing has changed, yet nothing is the same. We conquer sorrow, not by vanquishing it but by befriending it. The end is not yet, but the end is love, and even now love grows out of sorrow. That is God's way. The way of the cross.

We could spend forever meditating upon the mental suffering of Christ, the psychology of the passion. Every aspect of mental and emotional pain is to be found somewhere in his experience. I have time to look at only a few of them. First of all, there was the withering experience of rejection: "You will all fall away." He had, of course, already been rejected by his countrymen. The multitudes that followed him turned into enemies because he would not conform to their expectations. "Be our king, do it our way, lead us against our enemies." Those he had loved and sorrowed over, healed and fed, comforted and even entertained, turned against him. "What shall I do with the man you call King of the Jews?" "Crucify him, crucify him." There is evidence that even his family turned against him. Certainly they did not understand him, thought

him out of his mind, deranged, unhinged. Mary was there at
the end, we know, and a few brave women, but there is nothing
in the Gospels to suggest they understood the meaning of the
way he had to go. They were dumbly loyal, but they almost
certainly implored him to think again. Worst of all was the
rejection of his little chosen band. "You all will fall away." And
they did, even the bold and impulsive Peter: "I tell you, I know
not the man." Not *Jesus*, not *Lord*, not *Master*, not *Rabbi* but—
the man! He was *rejected*. In that experience of rejection was
the pain of every outcast, every loveless child, every shuffling
derelict. In that agony of abandonment was the rage and anguish of every psychotic who feels baffled by the nameless
waves of hostility that engulf him and overwhelm his sanity.
He was rejected. Try to enter into that experience, you who
are loved and valued and affirmed. Allow yourself to feel the
intolerable isolation of absolute rejection. And there is one final
note you should not miss. This Jesus, this man in whom God
was, felt rejected, abandoned by God. God in some sense forsook himself! He entered so deeply into the reality of human
abandonment that he experienced God-forsakenness. "My God,
my God, why hast thou forsaken me?" That, too, is a common
human experience: to feel that the whole universe is against
you, menaces you with cold malevolence. There is nowhere to
go, no one to whom to turn, no comfort anywhere, no prayer
answered, no plea heard. All is silent and black: God forsaken
in no-man's-land. Christ felt that, too. He knew the acute anxiety of the man who cannot believe, who can find nothing to
give meaning to his life. He knew the darkness because it swallowed him. He was rejected.

And he was in great fear and sorrow. There has always
been a tendency to dehumanize Christ, to make him into a
divine play-actor miming our condition upon the stage of history, but not really experiencing it. That is not consistent with
the truth of Christ as either man or God. However you treat
the paradox of Christ's nature, you must never forget that,
though God was in him, he had emptied himself in order precisely to be the victim of our humanity. And the record states
that in Gethsemane Christ was filled with a horror that almost
stopped his heart: "He began to be greatly distressed and troubled. And he said to them, 'My soul is very sorrowful, even to

death.' " Imaginative people suffer in anticipation more than
others, they feel in advance what is coming upon them. We
ourselves talk about "an agony of suspense." There was, doubtless, something of that in Christ's mind. He would be familiar
with the systematic barbarism of a Roman crucifixion. The
Romans made sure that everyone knew the details. It was their
great deterrent policy. Palestine well knew the sight of a man
slowly dying on a cross. So there was anticipatory fear: something of the same fear that grips a man as he is led into the
torture chamber in some steamy South American prison;
something of the fear that grips a woman after a double mas-
tectomy when she is told that her cancer is on the move again;
something of the fear that grips a man when the doctors whis-
per mysteriously at the foot of his bed and then palm him off
with a cheery vagueness; something of the fear that must clutch
the heart of a kidnap victim—perhaps a child—who is kept
blindfolded and bound in a basement by abductors whom she
has never seen and who tell her nothing. The 20th century
has invented many subtle modifications of fear. Terrorism, after
all, is a word we only recently invented. Terrorism: defined by
the *Oxford English Dictionary* as "a policy intended to strike with
terror those against whom it is adopted." Christ was brave but
he was not nerveless: he was struck with terror.

But there was another element in the psychology of the
passion. Any parent knows something of the anxiety that great
love brings: children you would die for are in great danger,
and you can only stand and watch from afar. What is happening to them is also happening to you. Your whole life becomes
a single focus of misery as you gaze, impotently, upon their
struggle to live; or as you wait to hear from the police if they
have been found. You *become* sorrow. It takes you over. It dom-
inates every waking and sleeping moment. There was that in
Christ's sorrow, for he was overwhelmed by the world's sorrow.
He came from the heart of the Father who gazes in anguish
upon the sufferings of his children. The church has always
mysteriously known that Christ in Gethsemane felt not only
the horror of his own passion but the accumulated horror of
human history. Like a thick cloud it blotted him out. Like a
rank mist it filled his lungs. Like a mighty and pitiless wave it
engulfed him. It all fell upon him in a dark and awful horror:

"My soul is very sorrowful, even unto death." That is a weight and scale of sorrow that we can enter only in a tiny way. We know something of the terrors of history, but only a fraction: God knows all, and that all—what Paul calls "the exceeding sinfulness of sin"—almost killed him before the first nail found its flesh.

Terror and loneliness, rejection and heartbroken sorrow are probably more terrifying modes of pain than certain types of physical suffering. But there are certain types of torture and disease that induce a level of pain which it is, apparently, almost impossible to imagine. The secret police of our totalitarian century have been highly creative in refining unendurable pain. The practitioners of that gruesome fraternity boast that there is no one whom they can't break down with a judicious blend of psychological and physical torture. Even as you read this, someone is screaming in agony as the experts work him over with dispassionate professionalism. Christ is crucified till the end of time. And man's old enemy, disease, is still able to torment us with pains that almost drive the sufferers mad. I understand that some of the pains of terminal cancer can, if not moderated by skillful and compassionate medication, produce an intensity of pain which is indescribable. As we seek to enter imaginatively into the pains of Christ, therefore, we must bring all these sufferers with us, for they, too, are part of the strange fabric of Christ's passion. In this way they make up what is lacking in Christ's suffering, in Paul's mysterious phrase.

While the psychology of the passion may be newer territory for meditation, the physical aspects of the suffering are so well known to Christians that there is a danger that they'll be passed over with a sort of liturgical breeziness. The Gospels, anyway, describe it all with great reticence and brevity. Let us, however, listen to the old, old story again and try to enter at least the fringes of the experience. We are told, quite simply, that "when they were come to the place which is called Calvary, there they crucified him." We ought to know something of what lies behind those momentous words.

Remember, then, that our Lord had not slept for almost two days. Keeping a man without sleep for an indefinite period is a necessary prelude to any effective torture. We know that

Jesus was in the Garden of Gethsemane all night, praying in an agony of fear and indecision. In the middle of the night they came for him. Again, there's nothing very unusual in this. Secret police always make their arrests at night. The night is congenial to them. In Hitler's Germany the Jew would lie abed waiting for the slamming of the car door, the pounding of feet on the stair, the smash of a shoulder against the door. Then the "via dolorosa," the ride in a car to a dreary building in the center of town. The first step on a trip to hell. Jesus was arrested in the middle of the night. According to the Gospels he was dragged through six trials in the hours that followed. He was taken before Annas, the father-in-law of Caiaphas the high priest, the power behind the Temple establishment; then he was taken to Caiaphas himself; then he was taken before a hastily and probably illegally summoned meeting of the Sanhedrin, the high court of the Jews; next there was the first trial before Pilate, who sent him to Herod; and again he was sent back to Pilate for the final sentence. During these hours he was beaten up at least twice. St. Luke tells us that "The guards who had Jesus in custody flogged him and made him the victim of their horseplay," and St. John tells us that, after Jesus had replied to a question from the high priest, "one of the Temple police who was standing by gave him a slap across the face." (Every society needs police, but they are easily brutalized by the job society gives them to do.) During those trials Jesus, we read, was bound. His arms were probably pulled tightly back behind him and roped painfully to his body. Immediately after Pilate had passed the sentence of death on Jesus, he sent him to be scourged, for scourging was always the prelude to crucifixion. There were few more painful ordeals than a Roman scourging. The victim was first stripped, and then either tied to a pillar in a bent position with his back exposed so that he could not move, or stretched rigid upon a frame. The scourge was made of leather thongs studded with sharpened pellets of lead or iron and pieces of bone. It literally ripped a man's back to pieces. According to Professor Barclay,

> Many lost consciousness under the lash; many emerged from the experience raving mad; few were untied from their bonds with spirit still unbroken.

Jesus suffered all this. In silence. Next, according to Matthew,

> Then the soldiers of the governor took Jesus into the
> praetorium, and they gathered the whole battalion before
> him. And they stripped him and put a scarlet robe upon
> him, and plaiting a crown of thorns they put it on his
> head, and put a reed in his right hand. And kneeling
> before him they mocked him, saying, "Hail, King of the
> Jews!" And they spat upon him, and took the reed and
> struck him on the head. And when they had mocked him,
> they stripped him of the robe, and put his own clothes
> on him, and let him away to crucify him (Matthew
> 27:27-31).

That's what we call ragging or bullying, and it combines both
psychological and physical torture. Sometimes what we call
teasing is only a refined version of the same kind of sadism. It
can happen anywhere: on school playgrounds; in family living
rooms; in offices; on factory floors; in army barrack rooms.
There are always those who get some sort of sexual gratifica-
tion out of this kind of thing, but most of those who engage
in it are small people who find an obscure importance in following some bully's attack upon the weak or the different. If
you've ever had a child bullied at school you'll know something
of the sadness and sickness of it all. In that scene in that army
square are set all the helpless victims of every bully in history:
the little Jewish child with a large star of David sown hastily
onto his jacket, dragging himself to school and the twisted
hatred of his classmates; the child with a funny accent or man-
nerism or disfigurement; a man or a woman from a sexual or
racial minority, jeered at and parodied by their coarse work-
mates; the endless permutations of victimization.

Then there began the procession to the place of execution. This always followed the same pattern. The criminal was
placed in the center of a hollow square of four Roman soldiers;
in front walked a herald carrying a board whitened with gypsum, the mineral from which plaster of Paris is made, with the

charge painted in black letters upon it. Jesus' charge read:

"This is Jesus of Nazareth, the King of the Jews."

That was Pilate's bitter little joke. The board was later fixed to
Jesus' cross. The criminal was taken to the place of crucifixion
by the longest possible way, by the busiest streets, and through
as many of them as possible, so that he might be a dreadful
warning to any others who might be contemplating some crime;
and, as he went, he was lashed and goaded. The modern equiv-
alent to that kind of public exposure would be, I suppose, the
hysterical coverage of an enraged press and television, flocking
around some victim like vultures. I think that it is important
to remember here that Jesus was not just bearing the sufferings
of the just or the innocent. Much of the suffering that men
and women endure is, in some sense, self-inflicted. That is why
society takes such a morbid interest in the tragedies of those
who commit some great sin or crime: it gives them license to
gloat over sins that infest their own heart. The victims of this
unedifying modern ritual are stripped of all privacy and paraded before the whole nation, just as Christ was dragged
through the streets of Jerusalem.

The criminal was forced to carry at least part of his own
cross. It is probable that the upright beam of the cross was
already in place in its socket on the hill of Calvary and Jesus
had to carry the cross-beam. When they reached the place of
execution, the cross was assembled and laid on the ground and
the criminal was thrown backward on it. At this point it was
customary to give the victim a drink of medicated wine mixed
with gall, to help to drug him for the pain that was to follow.
Matthew tells us that Jesus refused it:

. . . They offered Jesus drugged wine mixed with gall to
drink. Jesus tasted it and refused to drink.

Halfway up the upright beam of the cross there was a project-
ing ledge of wood, called the saddle, on which part of the
weight of the criminal's body rested, or the weight would have
torn the nails clean through his hands. As the criminal was

stretched upon the cross, the nails were driven through his hands. At that moment most victims cursed and swore and shrieked and spat at their executioners. Luke tells us that Jesus prayed:

> "Father, forgive them; for they know not what they do."

Usually only the hands were nailed, the feet being loosely bound to the upright beam of the cross. And the criminal was stripped of everything save a loincloth.

In a sense, then, it was all over. The action was past. Now one just waited for the end. We read, "And sitting down they watched him there." Jesus was crucified about 9 a.m., and he hung on the cross for six hours. He died about three in the afternoon. That was unusual. The real terror of crucifixion was that it was a lingering death. A man might hang on the cross for days, tortured by flies, parched with thirst, burned by the sun by day and frozen by the frost by night. Most victims died raving mad after days of unendurable agony. If a man refused to die or begged to be put out of his misery, it was the custom to pound him to death with the blows of a mallet. On this occasion, too, the authorities were in a hurry. The sabbath was at 6 p.m., and the bodies had to be removed before that. Jesus seems to have died after only six hours. In Luke's Gospel, before he dies Jesus utters a last prayer. He prayed the first prayer that every Jewish boy was taught to pray by his mother before the lamps were extinguished and he went to bed:

> "Father, into thy hands I commend my spirit."

He prayed the prayer our Lady had taught him when he was a little boy, then he bowed his head and died.

It was then that the authorities requested the soldiers to finish off the victims because the sabbath was near. John tell us:

> Since it was the day of Preparation, in order to prevent the bodies from remaining on the cross on the sabbath (for that sabbath was a high day), the Jews asked Pilate that their legs might be broken, and that they might be

taken away. So the soldiers came and broke the legs of the first, and of the other who had been crucified with him; but when they came to Jesus and saw that he was already dead, they did not break his legs. But one of the soldiers pierced his side with a spear, and at once there came out blood and water (John 19:31-34).

In one sense, the long siege of pain was over; in another sense, however, it was only just beginning. The dying goes on, the pain is never at an end. Jesus told us, "My Father worketh still, and I work." And it is the same work: the redemption of pain and sorrow by bearing it.

When Christians talk about "the problem of suffering" or "the problem of evil" they don't usually mean the *private* difficulty that faces someone who has, say, been told he has terminal cancer. The *problem* of suffering is more usually thought of as the philosophical problem posed by the existence of suffering and evil in a universe created by a God of love. The question that is asked is "How can you account for all this suffering if you say God is love?" It is, therefore, a problem for a certain kind of faith. Obviously, if you believed in an evil god, suffering would not be a problem: it would be a logical extension of your faith, it would follow from it. The problem for Christians arises because they believe that God is love, yet this child has just been tortured to death by a drunken and sadistic stepfather; God is love, yet this man in the very prime of his life, with many people dependent upon him, is struck down by a tumor of the brain; God is love, and so often the healers, the helpers of mankind, like Jesus of Nazareth, are cynically destroyed by cruel men. That is the problem, at least in the abstract. It is, of course, marvelously concentrated if you are told that you have a terminal disease or if you see your child killed or if you are dragged from your family in the middle of the night never to see them again. What does it mean? Why, God, why?

C. S. Lewis tried to establish that the problem of suffering is not increased by its numerical quantification. If ten men are dying of the same painful disease, there is not ten times more suffering in that ward than in the single room next door where one lies. You don't increase suffering by adding together everyone's suffering. Suffering is always only measurable in individual terms. If you could reduce suffering to one man it would still be a problem, but, according to Lewis, you have not increased the problem by adding together all the individual suffering. There is no calculus of pain. You don't increase it in real terms by multiplying instances, because it is always a private experience. By heaping up examples of pain you don't increase the problem. I'm not entirely satisfied with Lewis's point, but it does, I think, have value. You may not increase the quantity of suffering by adding all the individual instances, but you do, I think, increase the problem posed by it: you increase the culpability of God. If I have ten children and I neglect one, it may be held that there are extenuating circumstances, or that I can yet learn to mend my ways. If I neglect seven of them, surely my guilt has increased sevenfold, even if their pain is only measurable in single units. It is the sheer size and scope of suffering and evil that rises to accuse God. "What have you been doing while all this has been going on?" What *is* God doing about suffering and evil?

Well, I don't think the New Testament offers us a neat theory, though it has provided thinkers with unending material for their own interpretations. God did not answer mankind's plea with an argument, with a set of propositions, but with what Julian of Norwich would call "a showing," a revelation. We are given, not a theory but a poem, a picture, or a symphony, something that answers to the heart. And it's the heart, anyway, that needs to know, with that peculiar kind of heart knowledge that satisfies all the deep places of our nature. What are we shown in the New Testament? I want to try to answer that question by looking at three remarkable prophecies of his own death which Jesus uttered before the event. Mind you, these prophecies are not meant to be taken as magical exercises in precognition. That is never the meaning of biblical prophecy. God is not satisfying our curiosity about the future when he sends prophets to us. A prophet tells us what is coming to pass so that when it does come to pass we'll understand what it means, we'll see the hand of God in the event.

Let us think, then, about these three predictions of his passion. The first is in Mark 8:31:

And he began to teach them that the Son of man must suffer many things, and be rejected by the elders and the chief priests and the scribes, and be killed. . . .

The second comes in chapter 9, verse 31:

He was teaching his disciples, saying to them, "The Son of man is delivered into the hands of men, and they will kill him."

The third prophecy is in chapter 10, verse 33:

"Behold, we are going up to Jerusalem; and the Son of man will be delivered up to the chief priests and the scribes, and they will condemn him to death. . . ."

Each of these prophecies was uttered while Jesus with his disciples was making his last journey up to the Holy City. I want you to note the progression in the tenses in these three prophecies: The Son of man *must* suffer. Later on, the Son of man *is* delivered into the hands of men. Finally, in Jerusalem the Son of man *will be* delivered up.

The Son of man *must* suffer, it is necessary that he suffer, it is laid upon him. Then, a little later, the Son of man *is* delivered, *now;* the necessity has now overtaken him, he is already delivered over to his fate, and all this before he had entered Jerusalem, before a hand is laid upon him, before an order has been sent out to arrest him. He cannot, at this stage, be referring to the authorities in Jerusalem: he had not yet been delivered up, handed over by them. It is true that you can see the inevitability of it on the human level, but that is not what he's referring to. The necessity lies deeper than that. Who, if it is not the Jerusalem authorities, is the agent behind this necessity? Who is handing him over, even now? There can be only one answer: God. The death of Jesus was not just a humanly contrived crime; it was an act of God. God, Jesus was saying, has decided upon, has seen the necessity of, my death. The Son of man *must* suffer. He feels in his very depths the divine decision: it must be made. Later, he feels the decision has been made: the Son of man *is* delivered. The wheels are set in motion—not by Caiaphas and Pilate and Herod, but by God. Only when that level of divine necessity has been established is there a prophecy of the human action that will soon follow: we are going into Jerusalem and the Son of man *will be* handed over. Baffled as it was by the fact, the New Testament is quite convinced that the death of Jesus was the act of God. The Acts of the Apostles calls it "the determinate counsel and foreknowledge of God." God had decided that Jesus must die. There is horror in that necessity, and many of the theories built upon it have been scarcely moral: God wanted a victim to satisfy his angry vengeance upon humankind's sinfulness, and only Jesus would do. There was none other good enough.

But that is far from the heart of the New Testament, because it goes on to set forth an even more baffling claim. God was the agent, the plotter, the strategist behind the death of Christ, but he was also the victim of his own plot, the agent through whom it came to pass. The New Testament writers, in a glorious struggle with the meaning of Christ, taught that there was no separation between God and Christ. God was not using Christ, because God was in Christ, as Paul put it. God was not manipulating Jesus Christ, because what God was *he* was. By the time St. John's Gospel was written the identification was complete, the recognition was absolute, the message was finally and fully understood: "He that hath seen me hath seen the Father." In John it becomes quite explicit, but it is scarcely less explicit in Paul, the earliest material in the New Testament, and it is set forth with stark clarity in the opening words of the first Gospel: "The beginning of the Gospel of Jesus Christ, the Son of God." So the gap between God and that great question that resounds throughout man's sorrow is closed. There is now no distance between God and his suffering children. The victims no longer need cry out to the man above, because he is now himself the Victim. He is not on the other side of the barbed wire. He is not outside the broken heart. He is not the inviolate dispenser of remedies for our sickness. He is, in Eliot's strange phrase, "the wounded surgeon." God is God's victim.

How can we unravel that baffling conundrum? Not very much with our minds, I'm afraid, though the poets and the lovers and the great heartbroken preachers know what it means. Above all, it is the prophets who take us to the heart of it all.

Prophets are not men who dream up fantastic visions of the future. They are men through whom the passion and pain of God are communicated to men and women. In some sense, through them God's heart becomes transparent, his nature is disclosed, and what is disclosed is anguish as well as anger. The technical name for this is revelation, disclosure, unveiling. In the passion of the prophets the veil that hangs between God and humankind is lifted for an instant. Better still, it is like a muddy and sluggish river which suddenly runs over rocks and stones, and we see the water cleansed and made clear and the riverbed made visible. Whatever image you use, in the prophets you get, not words about God made up by men, but the very nature of God, in some way disclosed. You get, not theory but passion. And that passion is caused by the sorrows of the innocent, the contempt of the poor, the victimization of the weak. Through his servants the prophets God sets out to show the children of men what their world looks like, feels like, from God's point of view. He urges them to repent, to let compassion pour down like a cleansing torrent and justice like a mighty stream, to rid the earth of all oppression and wrong. And it always fails, always. The prophets are always rejected and persecuted.

> "O Jerusalem, Jerusalem, killing the prophets and ston-
> ing those who are sent to you! How often would I have
> gathered your children together as a hen gathers her
> brood under her wings, and you would not!" (Matthew
> 23:37).

The anguish of God speaks through the words of Christ. The endless defeat of God. And so sin and evil and suffering and guilt build up into a great lump, a prodigious cancer, a vast fibrous growth that distorts and destroys God's good creation, pressing upon each of us. It is no longer a matter of individual sin, of private peccadillos. It is all heaped together into a vast collective flood of racial and social misery, a *"massa peccata"* as the Fathers called it. Jung talked about the collective uncon-scious, that vast reservoir of forces beyond our control that pumps into our conscious and dreaming minds ideas and im-ages of hate and fear and bitterness and resentment, creating social stress, mental and emotional disease, and wave after wave of loneliness and alienation. From it human monsters lurch forth who seem to capture the evil genius of a generation, hideous caricatures of the evil that forms man in its own image. In the prophetic ministry of Christ this hideous army of the night is battled against. As you read the Gospels, particularly Mark, again and again you are given glimpses of the enormous anguish of Christ as he battles, alone, against this invasive force of evil and sorrow. He heals the sick, the maimed, the blind; but only a few of them among so many. He comforts the outcast and rejected; but only a few of them. He feeds the hungry in a world of hunger. He challenges hypocrisy and cruelty in a society built upon them. He casts out demons who have penetrated to the inner nature of human beings. In him God wages a war against the evil that has taken over his creation, an evil that men and women no longer even recognize, an evil they collaborate with or simply learn to live with, the way the rich live with the disturbing reality of the poor, by simply banishing them from their consciousness. And Christ fails, too. By one of those breathtaking inversions of value that characterize the sick mind of humanity, Christ is accused of being an evildoer. "He hath a demon. He casts out Beelzebul *by* Beelzebul." His good deeds are evidence of evil power. He is a sinner. (And we've all done it, haven't we? In the face of a goodness that challenges us, how often have we diminished it by questioning its motive? "What does he get out of it, I wonder? What's he compensating for, anyway?" And so we chip away at the challenge and end by calling good evil, because we have long, long since made evil our good.) That's what they did to Christ and, by the logic of extension, that's what they did to God. They turned value upside down. "If that's what God is like, let's get rid of him. Let us, for ever, remove this goading, challenging, probing tyranny of goodness. 'Evil be my good.'" And goodness goes to the cross. Goodness is defeated. This is the death of God. (It is interesting that George Steiner, the brilliant Jewish polymath, uses the same logic to account for the ferocious resentment against Jews that has characterized Western history and especially Hitler's "final solution": The Jews, he says, continue to represent the demand of God, his otherness. They stand outside the gate as a witness against our evil. They are the word of God set against every pride of human evil. So we turn against them and try to purge them from our midst. We try to liquidate them, banish them forever from before our eyes. This, too, is the death of God.)

Where are we left, then? We have turned against God our Father and crucified him. And God consents. Becomes, freely, our victim. But what has he achieved? What has he won by that magnificent defeat? Well, in those questions the tense is wrong, for it is not over yet. It is, of course, yet it is not. The cross is dismantled and Christ lies in his tomb. Yet the cross stands still, over against time until time runs out, because God is crucified until time's end. This surely is part of the meaning of that tree that stands still upon that hill: God is engaged with evil and sorrow until their final overthrow, and his tactics are the tactics of transfiguration. Let me try to explain that, though I don't entirely understand it myself.

In most of the martial arts the combatant is taught how to use his opponent's aggression as a weapon against him. By mastering a discipline of split-second timing he learns how to convert the attacking energy of the enemy into his own defense. That image goes partway toward explaining God's tactics of suffering and defeat: evil turns upon God and spends itself upon his heart, because God will bear all things, endure all things in order to save his children. He defeats us, not with the weakness of power but with the power of weakness. I have never once been saved from sin by a mighty intervention of God. I have sometimes been able to turn away from sin because I have caught sight of the crucified Christ, his face ravaged with love of me. What damns me as I sin is that love I cannot flee from. That's what defeats me, as one day I believe it will be shown to have defeated the whole mystery of evil. Then we shall see that not one tear has been wasted, not one pain has gone unfelt, not one sorrow has been lost. All of them, by the transfiguring love of God in Christ, will have been burned by his eternal sorrow into glory. "You now have sorrow, but I will see you again and your heart will rejoice, and your joy no man will take from you."

CHAPTER SEVEN

The God Who Conquers Death

Guilt is very common after a death. There is no chance after a death to make up for neglect or misunderstanding. There is no possibility now of that visit we never got around to, that talk about the old days; no way of clearing up the misunderstanding that clouded the last years of the relationship. The things we never had time for, the things we kept promising to get around to, are still undone. All the joys and unspoken tenderness we had stored up for that day when we'd have time . . . now we hear he's dead, and they're all still undone, still locked up in our mind; good-natured intentions that will never see the light, because he's gone. Now the guilt wells up. The futile regret for all the opportunities missed, even in a long life; the strange feeling that we never really showed him how much we loved him or admired him or owed him. Where, then, did all the time go? He was beside me all my life and I never quite got around to knowing him. Now he's beyond my reach. There was something I was just going to say—and he's gone. I missed him by seconds at an appointed place. Yes, guilt is very common after death, for who has ever really given himself completely to another in life? Who is not left with so much unsaid, so much undone, gestures that were never made, flowers that were never given? Who is not left without an aching regret at the death of one he loved, but not well enough?

Certainly not our Lord's friend, Joseph of Arimathea. Think of the keenness of his regret, the weight of his guilt. John tells us that he was a secret disciple of Jesus—secret, for fear of the Jews. Think of the burden of that regret, regret for a love he could not or would not show publicly, for fear. And there was more. Joseph was a councillor, a member of the Sanhedrin, the high court of the Jewish people, the body which condemned Jesus to death at dawn that Friday morning. Was Joseph there, sitting in anguished silence in that vehement assembly? We hear of no word spoken against the sentence, no courageous minority report, no dissenting opinion from one of the judges, no voice but the voice that cried "Crucify." Joseph of Arimathea. Doubtless he'd promised to declare himself one day, when the time was ripe. He'd stand up and be counted when the time came. Any day now he'd declare himself . . . but wait, the high priest is speaking: "Need we call further witnesses? You have heard the blasphemy. What is your opinion? What is your opinion, Joseph?" The record clearly states that the decision of the court was unanimous: sentence of death was passed on Jesus called the Christ. The sentence was duly carried out.

And Joseph, like all men who ever were, prepared with regret to bury one whom too late he loved. He poured all his guilt and regret into an expensive tomb. And his friend, another secret disciple, brought half-a-hundredweight of spices and herbs. It was the Jewish custom to wrap the bodies of the dead in linen cloths and to put sweet spices between the folds of the linen. Between them, Joseph and Nicodemus gave Jesus the burial of a king. They tried to purge their regret, as many have done, with an expensive funeral.

Poor Joseph of Arimathea, we can't leave him there in the spiced tomb, lovingly purging his regret over the broken body of his Lord, because his story does not end there. Joseph of Arimathea, who sat in silence for fear of the Jews while Jesus was condemned to death, became, according to Christian legend, a missionary. Tradition has it that in the year 61 he was sent to England by the Apostle Philip. He came to a place called Glastonbury. With him, the legend says, he brought the cup that was used at the Last Supper, and in it the blood of Christ. That cup became the Holy Grail, which it was the dream of King Arthur's knights to find. When Joseph arrived in Glastonbury, they say that he drove his staff into the ground to rest on it in his weariness, and that the staff budded and became a bush which blooms every Christmas Day. St. Joseph's thorn still blooms in Glastonbury, and the first church in all England was built there, where it is still a center for Christian pilgrims.

It is a legend, of course, but it has a certain usefulness and validity. Joseph, though we know little about what happened to him after his labors on Passover Eve, represents the extraordinary nature of the beginning of the Christian church. We have to ask ourselves what it was that transformed Joseph, the silent, fearful, guilt-ridden man of Good Friday, into *Saint* Joseph, the missionary of Christian legend. It was the same power which reclaimed Peter after his bitter denials and sent him, after many labors, to death on a cross; it was the same power which sent Thomas, the doubter, as apostle to India; it was the same power which changed a tattered bunch of deserters who fled in fear from the Temple police in the strange half-light of Gethsemane Garden into a band of men and women who faced the Roman Empire itself and prevailed. It was the power of the Risen Christ. And be quite certain of the fact, be quite certain of the intolerable nature of the claim that is being made: that body which Joseph labored over with terrible regret on Friday afternoon rose in triumphant and unconquerable majesty three days later. That's the power and that's the fact which transformed Joseph of Arimathea and countless others. He rose again. And we don't mean the corpse was resuscitated to the same life as before, a bit more time bought, as we might buy time for a drowning man by the kiss of life. There are no parallels to this event: it is overpoweringly unique. A body was not simply revived—it was glorified, it was raised to a new and eternal level of being. This event imposes an intolerable strain upon our frail human vocabulary: there are no words to describe the unbearable glory of it, no parallels in our experience to which we can liken it. The only thing to which we can liken the Resurrection of Jesus Christ is the very creation of the universe. According to our faith God created the universe from nothing. God said "Let there be," and life and matter came into existence from nothing. This fact in itself is impossible to grasp. It is impossible for us, conditioned as we are, to think of Nothing, and to grasp the power and wonder of that first act of creation, that majestic "Let there be." We cannot know how it was, but we know it by its effects. We know it by its results, by the creation itself. And the Resurrection is a New Creation. It is another act of creative power by God. It is a new "Let there be."

Like all the historical claims of the Christian church, the Resurrection of Jesus from the dead has a double nature. It is based on facts, but facts will not convey the reality of the event by their own power. Behind the facts there is a revealed truth, an overture from God, and that "telegram from God," as one theologian puts it, can only be understood with the help of faith. By faith I mean that patient waiting upon the inner meaning of the event to disclose itself. Faith of this sort is far from being gullible credulity. It is based upon the premise that the human mind and heart can dispose themselves in such a way that God can address them, utter a word that will be heard by them. The irony is that God chooses to reveal himself through the highly ambiguous mediation of historical events and persons. "Is not this the *carpenter's* son?" As Mark tells us, you can see and see, and still not perceive; you can hear and hear, and still not understand. The faculty that discerns the divine overture can lie dormant within us, or it can be willfully suppressed. To those who believe, John tells us, to those who wait expectantly upon the action of God, the veil is lifted and we see the glory of God, though we never wholly possess or control it.

The Resurrection has to be approached on two levels, therefore. There is the level of fact and there is the level of meaning. People differ notoriously about the interpretation of facts; they even differ about the facts themselves. There are considerable differences of detail in the accounts in the New Testament of the facts surrounding the discovery of the Resurrection of Jesus. There is no attempt to provide a neat and orchestrated version of this controversial event. The New Testament writers and the early church must have been as aware of the differences in detail as we are. The absence of collusion is itself strong evidence of honesty in the first witnesses. There is no attempt to "cook the books." The differences, anyway, do not seriously affect the central claim. And I want, now, to rehearse the details of that central claim.

First of all, Jesus was quite definitely dead when they took him down from the cross. The Romans always made sure of that by pounding the victims with mallets to make sure they were dead if they stubbornly refused to die. When they came to Jesus they found that he was dead already. Just to make sure, they plunged a spear into his side, though they did not break his body with the mallet. From the earliest days some have claimed that Jesus had just gone into a swoon on the cross, and that he'd revived later in the coolness of the tomb where they laid him. (That, incidentally, is negative evidence of an important sort: people, you see, had to account for the startling fact that his body had disappeared.)

This brings me to the second fact. When his followers came to the tomb on the first day of the week, they found the tomb open and his body gone. All the Gospels agree with that fact. So, apparently, did the opponents of the Christian movement. The one thing no one was able to do was produce the body of Jesus. Had they been able to do that, the Christian Faith would have been scotched at birth. And we can be quite certain they tried to find it. Unsuccessful, they spread the story that the followers of Jesus had stolen his body and that the Resurrection was a cleverly concocted lie. The fact that the body of Jesus was never produced is enormously strong evidence. No one seems to have disputed the fact of the empty tomb. That, anyway, proved nothing. The controversy raged over how the tomb came to be empty. The followers of Jesus claimed that he had risen from the dead. No sane, logical magistrate was going to accept that. They concluded, circumstantially, that his body must have been stolen. No one seems to have challenged the central claim, that the body was missing.

The third fact is less straightforward, but it is fundamental. You have to ask yourself: Were the disciples of Jesus capable of pulling off such a massive hoax? The question is complicated by a further question: What did they expect to gain from such an outlandish claim? It brought them nothing but persecution and derision. To maintain a lie like that in the face of universal scepticism you have to achieve an impossibly high degree of discipline among a very varied group of people, yet no one broke down, no one turned state's evidence and led the authorities to the body or gave an account of the planning of the fraud. Even more extraordinary is the change in the disciples. We are so used to making this point and hearing it expounded that the amazing surprise has gone out of it. Nevertheless, it is an extraordinary phenomenon. We know that his closest followers all forsook him. Peter, the leader, denied even knowing him only hours after his arrest. Yet weeks later the same Peter is proclaiming to the world an even more revolutionary allegiance; he is claiming that the man they unjustly crucified has been raised from the dead; and for his pains he was beaten and imprisoned. The same goes for the others. Is it credible to believe that these men, broken and demoralized by Good Friday, could have got together in the space of a few hours, hatched a plot around a claim that was intrinsically unbelievable, then pulled it off with such passionate courage? From what we know of them they were quite incapable of such imaginative mendacity. Paul is the strongest in his repudiation of the charge of dishonesty. Why, he asks, are we staking our lives on this claim, if we made it up ourselves? He says: "Why am I in peril every hour? I protest, brethren, by my pride in you which I have in Christ Jesus our Lord, I die every day! What do I gain if, humanly speaking, I fought with beasts at Ephesus? If the dead are not raised . . ." (1 Corinthians 15:31ff.). The hoax theory of the Resurrection requires more credulity than belief in the empty tomb.

The fourth fact is related to the third; it is the emergence of the church as a distinctive body within the Jewish nation, with its own courage and self-confidence. The Gospels are not sentimental about the disciples of Jesus. They tell us, on page after page, that the disciples did not understand Jesus and strongly disapproved of his interpretation of his vocation. They had wanted a conventional Messiah, a worldly leader. Jesus let them down: "We had hoped that he was the one to redeem Israel." He wasn't, apparently. He was yet another failure. They all fell away. Yet, soon they are confronting the world with the claim that this same Jesus is the One sent by God to redeem and save, and that he is not dead but alive and active and can be known now. Only an extraordinary event can account for that miraculous transformation. They locate that event on Easter Sunday, and the very keeping of the first day of the week by the first Christians is powerful proof that their claim is quite specific. The first disciples were devout Jews, strongly committed to sabbath observance. Yet soon the sabbath is hardly regarded at all. They are keeping the next day, the first day of the week, as the Day of Resurrection.

The fifth fact in this chain of evidence is the widely attested fact of the appearances. They are as central a part of the early evidence as the empty tomb. Paul lists them in chapter 15 of his First Letter to the Corinthians, written no more than twenty years after our Lord's death, when many of the original witnesses were still alive and available for questioning. (Twenty years is no time at all: I was ordained twenty years ago, and can remember every detail vividly—if the Risen Lord had appeared to me then I would certainly remember it clearly now!)

Now, each of these five elements on its own may not be persuasive, but cumulatively they are very powerful indeed. The final fact is the universal testimony of the church down the ages that Jesus is not dead. Countless Christians throughout the centuries have witnessed to the reality of Jesus, not only by their words but by their sacrificial lives and by their very deaths. In him they have found a relationship so strong and real that it has enabled them to deny the strongest urges of their created nature. No, people have never been able to disprove the Resurrection by the discovery of new evidence or by a convincing repudiation of the old. They have, instead, written it off in advance as intrinsically impossible.

Our problem as human beings is that we can know things in our own experience only from what has happened in our past. Bishop John Taylor says that we are like a man sitting in a boat drifting downstream with the current, so that our life is always flowing from behind. It is the past and our previous experience which guides our understanding. But what if we turned around and gazed upstream? We would then see things flowing toward us, not behind us. Meaning would come out of the future, not just out of the past. We would be disposed to see things coming to us from the future; we would not simply judge them by our own past experience. We have no experience of a resurrection—it is something completely new—so we tend to repudiate it; it is not part of what we have been. That way of looking at things renders us incapable of seeing or handling anything utterly new that God wishes to present before us: we will not believe though one were to rise from the dead.

But God does not want us to be the captives of the past in any way. He is the God of the future: he brings forth, from the treasure of his love, new things, beyond our understanding. "Behold, I am doing a new thing. Can you not perceive it?" The reason for much of the paralysis that grips both church and world today is that we are tired and cynical and jaded. The past has conditioned us. It has ironed all surprise and expectation out of us. The best is behind us. Nothing new can happen. The fire will never burn again. The Holy Spirit of God cannot stir from our dead embers any new flame of love or justice or achievement. The Resurrection of Jesus from the dead defiantly contradicts all that. It shows us a God who is ahead of us and our hopes: our God is not tired and run-down. To him belongs the future as well as the past. New days and new dawns await us. Our God has done a new thing. He is not bound by the tired sophistries of dead philosophers: he is ahead of us. The future beckons. Christ goes before us into new days, unto the very Resurrection of the dead.

The Resurrection of Jesus establishes Hope as a fundamental law of the universe. The nature of history is not bound forever to the iron rule of the past. New possibilities flow toward us from the future of God. Hope is trust for the future, the calm expectation that God lies ahead, even in death itself. The Resurrection is what theologians call "an eschatological event," from the Greek word for "end" or "what lies ahead." It is a preview of God's plan for his broken creation, an announcement, in the language of cinema, of God's "future presentation"; it is what's coming. Of course, it is difficult to live up to this theology of hope in the midst of the tragedies of history and the confusions of our personal lives. Nevertheless, it can be a transforming influence upon private lives and public events. The whole saga of God's continuing creation is based upon the reality of growth and the emergence of new possibilities. "Behold, I am doing a new thing," God tells us, and he calls us to a new courage; he calls us to live expectantly, even in the face of the overwhelming tragedies of time. The Christian church in time is called to live as an eschatological remnant, to live as though God's future were already realized in the present. Christians, here and now, are called to the life of future blessedness. They are to be signs, in time, of God's certain plan for the end of time. In the Sermon on the Mount Jesus gave us a description of that kind of life; he gave us, in those famous and wounding words, a sort of eschatological sketch, a picture of the beatitude which would characterize God's future kingdom. In the remainder of this book I want to attempt a brief, practical exposition of the character he there set forth. What does it mean for the Christian to live now according to the pattern of God's future? How can we attempt to live the life of future blessedness?

PART THREE

The Blessings
of the Future

CHAPTER EIGHT

The Sermon on the Mount

The block of material which, as far as I know, St. Augustine was the first to call the Sermon on the Mount, is found in Matthew's Gospel, chapters 5 to 7. A shorter version of the same material is found in St. Luke, chapter 6, and individual sayings from the material found in Matthew are found scattered in other parts of Luke. The first question we have to ask ourselves, therefore, is whether such a sermon as Matthew records was ever preached. We know that Matthew often collects sayings of Jesus and places them in sequence. Has he done that here? Has he just taken a lot of unconnected proverbs and linked them artificially together, or is he preserving, however loosely, an actual connected utterance of our Lord? As usual, the scholars differ. I think it is highly likely that our Lord did impart his teaching to his closest followers in a systematic way, though it is also likely that much of his teaching was repeated again and again in different contexts. The sermon as recorded by Matthew would have taken only about fifteen minutes to deliver. Along with some scholars, I think that the teaching that is embodied there was probably delivered in what we could think of as a sort of retreat, a period of intensive training. Matthew, therefore, is recording in a rather formal way teaching that might have been given over a longer period. These technical questions, however, do not really matter much. What matters enormously is that we have here a piece of sustained teaching which is gripping in its intensity, and which has captured the heart and imagination of history, though men and women have admired it far more than they have attempted to follow it.

The next question we must bring to it is whether our Lord had some specific purpose in mind when he delivered it. Scholars have often compared Matthew's account of this piece of sustained moral teaching with Moses' deliverance of the Ten Commandments to Israel. Both occasions are recorded as taking place in the mountains. In the case of Israel, God had just made a covenant or contract with Israel, and the law which Moses brought down from the Mount, the Ten Commandments, was Israel's part of that contract. They were to be a special people, an agent of God's saving purpose in the world, marked by their observance of a rigorous moral and social code. There are many parallels in what Jesus did. His intention seems to have been the formation of a new society in the world, a new Israel, which would embody his presence and live after his pattern. He chose, not twelve tribes, but twelve apostles, and he delivered, not ten commandments—blunt and straightforward pieces of law—but a profound and radical new program of character and conduct which would indeed set his chosen people apart from the rest of the world.

Well, then, is the Sermon on the Mount the Christian law code, as the Ten Commandments were the Jewish law code? In one sense the answer must be "yes," but we must immediately qualify it. "Law" is a word with several meanings. We talk of a law of nature, a scientific law. And we talk of the law of a nation, positive law. That kind of law is straightforward and fairly easy to understand and follow. If you break it, you are punished. The law we have in the Sermon on the Mount is not that kind of law at all. For one thing, no one will punish you if you break it. For another, it is not law in the direct sense of pointing to particular acts which it is wrong to commit. There is something of that in it, but it goes much deeper than that. It is a law which is not concerned only with what you do, but with what sort of character you have. It is concerned, for instance, not only about particular sexual acts, but about the very thoughts and intentions and longings of your heart. In other words, it is more concerned with the formation of character, with the deep intentions of your heart and mind, than with simple surface behavior. It is not concerned mainly with your outward conduct, but with the inner nature that leads to conduct. Our Lord said that a good tree produces good fruit and an evil tree evil fruit. What he is concerned about, therefore, is how we can be good through and through, so that our actions, our fruits, are automatically good because they come from a good nature. So this kind of law is more like the laws of nature than the law of the land, the criminal law. No authority will punish you if you break this law, because breaking this law leads, in the end, to its own punishment by an inevitable process. It is, if you like, more like the laws of health. No one sends you to prison if you overeat, or drink too much, or smoke sixty cigarettes a day and never take any exercise. But all the time you do these things you are offending against the law of your own health, and sooner or later you pay the price. So the Sermon on the Mount is about the way to spiritual and moral growth. You can ignore it if you like, but sooner or later you will pay the price.

So far my emphasis has been on the role of the individual in his own struggle after goodness. There is another part of the intention of Jesus which is just as important. John tells us that God so loved the world that he sent Jesus, his Son, into the world to save it. The implication is inescapable. The world is in danger. Left to itself it will plunge into darkness and chaos. Part of the purpose of the society Jesus established in the world was to prevent these things from happening. Early on in this sermon he delivers two of his most famous proverbs: "Ye are the salt of the earth" and "Ye are the light of the world." In the ancient world salt was not just a condiment, something you sprinkled on the fish and chips you wrapped up in the Jerusalem *Daily News*. It was far more important as a preservative, a disinfectant. It prevented decay. Again, the implication is clear. Christians exist in a world which is prone to moral and social and spiritual decay and corruption. We all know this, don't we? We ourselves feel the influence of the world's corrupt standards in all sorts of ways. They form us. They make us greedy and lustful and acquisitive. When that happens we are like salt that has lost its savor, its saltness, its ability to preserve and prevent corruption. Sometimes in excavating salt it would get mixed with gypsum or alkali. It would then be useless. Christians, too, can get mixed up in the world's standards, and they, too, lose their saltness. Instead of being in the world as agents of purification and preservation, holding up standards and ideals before a corrupt society, they can become mixed up with the world's standards. They are then useless, no longer fulfilling the purpose Jesus set for them. "If the salt have lost its savour, wherewith shall it be salted? It is thenceforth good for nothing, but to be cast out and trodden underfoot of men." Christians, therefore, are called upon to preserve their standards not just because they want to save their own souls, but because Jesus has given them an important ministry to the world. A surgeon is no good to his patient unless he carefully disinfects himself before operating. If he goes to his patients with dirty hands he will make them worse, not better. If Christians allow themselves to be taken over by the world's values they, too, become worse than useless to the world. So we are called by Jesus to be agents of purification, antiseptics in the midst of a diseased society.

And we are called to be lights. In the ancient world there was little public lighting in the streets. A city could be seen a long way off on the dark country roads because its houses were illuminated from within. It could not be hid. Christians are called to be lights, shining out in the moral darkness of a world that lurches closer to chaos every day. The light of the Christian is his conduct, his good works. We are called, says Jesus, to let our light shine before men, that they may see our good works, and glorify our Father who is in heaven. It is a cliché that a good life speaks louder than a good sermon. Christianity, they say, is caught, not taught. The saint is the best argument for the Christian message. When men and women see the light that shines out of a Mother Teresa in Calcutta, a light that cannot be hid, they ask themselves questions, they wonder that such light can burn in so dark a place. So, as the old mission hymn had it, Christians are not called to shine in their small corner unseen by the world, but to be like a city set on a hill, blazing with holiness and joy.

In giving us this teaching, therefore, Jesus was concerned to save and redeem his world, plunged in darkness, heavy with the sweet smell of decay. He called his followers to be salt and light, salt that would often burn in the world's torn flesh and light that would often blind its darkened eyes. In other words, we are called to be different, called to a special ministry. Often that means we must enrage and offend, but only for the world's sake. "Ye are the salt of the earth." "Ye are the light of the world."

When I read through the Sermon on the Mount, I am plunged into sorrow, despair, and remorse. When I compare that blazing standard with my own cowardice and corruption, I am near to tears. Who can live up to this impossible standard? Who can control his innermost desires and thoughts? Who can stop his innate longing for comfort and security? Who can easily bless those who curse him, and turn the other cheek to those who would smite him? How is it possible to begin to live up to this sublime ideal of sanctity? Are we, then, wasting our time in even thinking about it? Would it not be more honest simply to confess our impotence, our moral bankruptcy, and throw ourselves only on the mercy of God? Is it not enough to rely on God's forgiveness without attempting to follow in the heroic footsteps of Christ? We are not heroes and heroines. We are ordinary men and women. How can we live up to this impossible standard?

Well, again there have been a number of answers to that plea. Some scholars maintain that Christians were not meant to live up to this impossible standard, but that Jesus gave that teaching to a very special group of men for a particular time only. One scholar calls it "an interim ethic," meant to cover only the period of our Lord's life and immediately after his death, when his return was expected daily. Under those particular circumstances it was possible to sustain such heroism. It was a kind of martial law for a particular period of warfare, but people cannot live under martial law forever. They can sustain a heightening of effort for a short period, but they cannot live for long under such stress. So, they say, we are not meant to attempt it—or not all of it. It is like an examination paper on which we are asked to attempt only three questions, not the whole paper.

Other scholars have gone ever further. Jesus never meant anyone to observe it, they say. He was showing his disciples what real goodness was like in order to show them how impossibly far from goodness they were. He did it to reduce them to despair, to shatter their self-righteousness. Having seen just

how sinful and hopeless they were, they would then fall back
on the mercy and forgiveness of God, who demanded nothing
from them except repentance.

Others have taken a different line. Easy, they say. All it
takes is a bit of effort and concentration, and you'll manage it.
Just pull yourself together. Don't be defeatists, it's not that
difficult.

None of these approaches appeals to me as coming close
to the real intention of Jesus. Of course, we must begin by
recognizing just how terribly difficult and demanding it is.
Anyone who thinks the Christian life is easy is fooling himself.
Following Jesus is not like taking a leisurely Sunday stroll. It
is more like an Everest expedition. It requires discipline and
effort and heroism and sacrifice. There is much danger. It is
tempting to give up altogether. We won't get anywhere until
we recognize that. Yes, it is difficult, but not impossible. Not
impossible, if we recognize one absolutely fundamental thing:
we cannot do it on our own, by our own efforts. Jesus said that
unless a man be born again he cannot enter the kingdom of
heaven. We are called to be a new kind of human being, and
to be it we must go through a rebirth, a real change in our
hearts. We must be converted, turned around, made over. And
that is the work of the Holy Spirit. We'll never do it on our
own. We know how difficult it is to change ourselves. We know
how difficult it is just to learn to hold our tongue. How much
more difficult, then, to be completely remade, renovated, made
new. Difficult, but not impossible, because Jesus himself is with
us, leading us on, guiding us, helping us over the difficult
places. Without him, without an experienced guide, it would
be madness to attempt it, just as it would be madness to attempt
a serious mountain climb without expert help.

CHAPTER NINE

The Beatitudes

Annual income twenty pounds, annual expenditure nineteen nineteen six, result happiness. Annual income twenty pounds, annual expenditure twenty pounds ought and six, result misery.

So said Mr. Micawber, and thereby defined the precariousness of human happiness—in his day sixpence made the difference. The pursuit of happiness is a basic human preoccupation, and books on the subject still do brisk business. Bookshops are full of them. Fashions change, of course: a few years ago the emphasis was all on passivity and sexual athleticism. We were told not to do but to *be*, to let go, to relax. The model was some kind of laid-back flower child, always smiling, never aggressive, never worked up. It was Zen and the Eastern model. Near it on the rack were the books about achieving joy and happiness through sex, including Alex Comfort's book on the subject, offering a baffling series of complicated recipes, and laid out with all the appeal and subtlety of the *Good Food Guide*. The fashion has changed again. The happiness and fulfillment books these days are tougher: they're all about dieting and running and asceticism and assertiveness, but still they attempt to provide their readers with a quick route to human satisfaction. Jesus, at the beginning of his great sermon, offers us a quick sketch of the character of those who would follow *him*. He offers us, not a quick recipe for happiness, but a character sketch of the truly happy Christian. I said before that the pattern of behavior which emerges from the Sermon on the Mount is one that contradicts and contrasts with the world's way, and this contrast is made particularly vivid in the Beatitudes. The German philosopher Nietzsche said that Christianity was the transvaluation of all values, it challenged and turned around all the values of the world. If you take each beatitude and reverse it you'll see what he meant: blessed are the rich in this world's goods, for they think they own the earth; blessed are the self-satisfied because they never feel depressed, and so on. But let's look now at these seven characteristics of the truly blessed and happy person.

Blessed are the poor in spirit

The word "poor" in the Bible is a code word; its meaning is loaded. We immediately think of economic poverty, and that is part of the flavor of the word, but there is obviously much more to it. Poverty as such does not bring blessedness: some poor people are filled with envy and bitterness and resentment. Poverty of spirit is an inward disposition which may be best described as detachment. Job had it in abundance when he said, after the tragedies that befell him, "The Lord gave, and the Lord hath taken away; blessed be the name of the Lord." Detachment is a joyous but nonobsessional attitude to material things and even to other people. One appreciates them but is not wrongly dependent upon them. I suppose the psychologist would describe such a person as "secure." He or she does not need to bolster up an inner lack of esteem with a lot of material goods, nor do they manipulate or prey upon others. They are poor in spirit. They travel light. They are filled with laughter, they love the beauty of this world, but they know its real value is something that can never be taken away from them. But there is another note to this beatitude. In the Old Testament the poor were a special class of people who trusted in God because everything else had been taken from them. One might translate the word "the pious" or "the devout." These people have learned through bitter experience that nothing in this life can offer permanent support and security. All flesh is grass. All things come to an end. Everything that one holds dear can be wiped out in the blink of an eye. "The Lord gave, and the Lord hath taken away." The poor are those who are able to say, in spite of their agony of loss, "Blessed, blessed is the name of the Lord." The person who is poor in spirit, in other words, lives permanently in the attitude that most of us might achieve on our deathbed: as everything falls away from us and life itself ebbs out, reality will be reduced to the waiting and expectant presence of God. With Job we'll say, "Naked I came from my mother's womb, naked I shall return. The Lord gave, and the Lord hath taken away; blessed be the name of the Lord." "Blessed are the poor in spirit, for even now they are in the kingdom of God."

Blessed are those who mourn, for they shall be comforted

If you were beginning to gain the impression that the true Christian was a chilly, unemotional character, marked by an aloof detachment, this second beatitude will put you straight. Mourning is not something that characterizes the stiff-upper-lip brigade, but it is something, apparently, which should characterize the Christian. Again, there are several layers of meaning in this beatitude, but the first point I want to make is a general one. Many people in our society have been trained not to show emotion because it is not manly. They have been forced to bury their emotions beneath blocks of subconscious ice because they have been wounded or rejected somewhere in the past. Either experience can produce a type of person who is emotionally refrigerated: they never really feel anything, or they won't admit to themselves that they feel anything. They are always in control. They are measured and efficient and machinelike in their responses. In fact, the poor dears are not really entirely human. Part of them has never been properly born, or has never been allowed to grow. Such people can feel very isolated, baffled by their inability to feel, to break down and cry, or throw their hats in the air and do a somersault for very joy. That kind of person is not the character described in the Beatitudes. The second beatitude tells us that those who follow this sermon must *mourn*. Mourning is a deep sense of loss which wells up through the heart in an almost unbearable emotion of sorrow. If you have ever truly mourned the death of someone you love, been wracked by spasms of grief that

simply take over the body and convulse it, you'll know what I
mean by mourning. Nowadays doctors are telling us again what
ancient wisdom has always known, that such mourning after
a death is absolutely essential if the bereaved person is to re-
cover from the death. If he does not go through this process,
either because he represses it or because he is drugged by his
physician to muffle the pain, he is storing up problems for
himself. We need to mourn. It is natural after a death. It is
fitting. Our emotions are part of us. They help to cleanse us.
They help us to cope with tragedy and loss. Deny them and
you damage your mental and emotional health.

But Christians are called to mourn much more than the
death of those they love. They are, first of all, called upon to
mourn their own sinfulness. In these jaunty and self-confident
days it is thought to be a bit neurotic to think about or even
admit to sin. Well, there is an unhealthy preoccupation with
sin, to be sure, but I don't think you can say our Lord had it.
As I meditate on the New Testament I gather from it increasingly a tremendous sense of the authority and strength of Jesus,
and also get a strong sense of his sanity and clarity. Unlike us,
there was nothing in him of that self-deception that blinds us
to our true nature. And our Lord, loving and forgiving though
he was, was utterly convinced of the evil that lies in every human heart. He called men and women to realism about themselves, to a recognition of their true nature and all its vast
potential for sanctity and for self-destruction.

Part of the problem with the kind of radical sinfulness he
was talking about was that, by definition, it carefully concealed
itself from its carriers like some kind of cunning parasite. But
you don't have to be a great philosopher to recognize this potential for self-deception that characterizes us. We are all splen-
did at recognizing the faults of others. Think how resistant we
are to any true admission of our own faults. One of our Lord's
best-known proverbs celebrates this ancient double standard.
He talked about the man who pointed out that his brother had
a speck of dust in his eye, while failing to notice that he had
a great plank of wood sticking out of his own eye. Think of
the celebrated examples of self-deception in history: think how
our forefathers in the faith traded in slaves from the West
African coast. Tradition has it that one of Victorian England's

best-loved hymns was written by the pious captain of a slaving ship, sitting on the deck while his grim cargo were dying in the hold below. That man had buried the truth of his own conduct so completely beneath his conscious mind that he was unaware of it. He was no more a monster than you or I, but he was utterly self-deceived. Or think about the German nation during the period of the Holocaust. Do you think they did not know what was going on? They drove the trains to the death camps, after all. They supervised the gas ovens. They painted the signs that disguised the obscene reality of the final destination. How did they live with it, pious Christians that many of them were? They did not admit it. They were able to detach themselves from what they did. They split themselves in two, the better to cope with the evil they practiced. They would go home to their nice wives and blonde children at night and be good husbands, singing grace, taking the family to church, while the Holocaust occupied their working hours. Extreme cases, you say? Yes, but they prove the point, because if human beings are able to disguise from themselves such monstrous evil so completely, you can be quite certain that they are even better at hiding from lesser evils. So we must be on our guard against self-deception. We must know ourselves through and through, and we must mourn not only for the sins we have committed, but for the basic instability of our character that leads to such conduct.

And remember, we are to *mourn*. Mourning is different from guilt. Mourning is the emotion of loss felt to an unbearable degree. That is what we are to feel: sorrow for some mysterious loss of innocence and integrity in our souls, sorrow for the wounded creatures we are. I would go further, I would describe it as a sort of pity—not self-pity, but pity for the self. In Hopkins' words: "My own heart let me more have pity on. Let me live to my sad self hereafter kind." The recognition of what we are is the very prelude to our being comforted, because it is this very state that Christ came to heal; but how can he, if we refuse to believe we have any need of his ministry?

So we mourn our own nature and its cross-grained, self-wounding, self-deceiving reality—but we mourn more than that. We are called to be world-mourners, we are called to what Hopkins called "a world-sorrow," a sorrow at the pains of children, the sufferings of the bereaved, the misery of the mentally ill, the tortures of the condemned and persecuted. Christians are called to feel the pain of God's world and to grieve over it. They are not to allow themselves to become apathetic, unfeeling, their emotions enameled over by too much stress. They are to weep and lament, to feel in their very hearts the sorrows that disfigure the world. Those who do this, those who have not buried their emotions, are described as happy by Jesus. There is only a contradiction here if your definition of happiness is too narrow. Happiness is not a shallow feeling of private well-being. Biblical happiness, blessedness, is a state of being, not just of feeling. It is a recognition that such a person is to be congratulated, is blessed, fortunate in the way he is, because he is then closest to God, who mourns his poor world's suffering. And it is one of the most profound paradoxes of the Christian life that those who mourn most deeply their own sin and the pain of the world find, through their sorrow, the comfort of God holding them even as they weep, and in sweeps the sense of God's ultimate victory, the certainty of his final cure. Such a person knows what Mother Julian meant when she said: "Sin is behovely, but all shall be well, and all manner of thing shall be well."

Blessed are the meek,
for they shall inherit the earth

The Greek word *praüs,* which is here translated "meek," means gentle, kind, courteous, considerate, forgiving. The word "meek" has a rather weak sense in English, but it is far from indicating a weak and feeble disposition in its possessor. If we look at its opposite we'll see why. The opposite of the meek or considerate or forgiving person is the bullying, vindictive, judgmental person. Paradoxically, these overbearing characteristics are usually the mark of the insecure, unhappy, inwardly uncertain person. You have probably noticed in yourself that you are usually loudest in your condemnation of others when you are on your weakest ground, probably even attacking something in them that is very much a part of your own makeup. A story might illustrate this. A famous preacher died, and someone was appointed to go through his sermons with a view to their publication. Very often he noticed a set of initials written in the margins at certain points in most of the scripts: AWS. The editor took the problem to the great man's wife. "What did these letters mean in all these sermons?" "Ah," she said, "Argument weak—shout!"

The ground of Christian meekness is found in two experiences, both related to the second beatitude, "Blessed are they who mourn." The Christian is a realist about himself. He knows his own nature, is honest about his own sinfulness. He knows far more about his sinfulness than any other human being, so he is not defensive and self-righteous about himself in the face of criticism and attack from others. He says to himself with a quiet smile, "They don't know the half of it—only God does." When he is wrongfully accused, therefore, he doesn't jump up and immediately start defending himself loudly. They may be wrong about this, he says, but if they really knew what I was like they'd really have something to go on about. So he accepts it all ruefully, quietly, strongly.

But there is something else he knows, too. Sinner he may be, worse sinner than the world knows, yet a forgiven sinner, a sinner whom God continues to love and accept. That gives him an enormous inner security—not, however, the security of self-righteousness, the false security of the humbug and the hypocrite, but the strong, unassailable security of the man who knows that God knows about him and yet accepts him—not because he is a plastic saint, but because, well, because God loves him. That inner security, based as it is upon self-knowledge, makes the Christian considerate of the weakness of others, patient with them, understanding, the very opposite of the moral bully.

Of course, that kind of attitude has always been very rare in the world. It stands out like a light in the darkness, like a city set on a hill. In the world men and women are always standing up for their rights, no matter who suffers. When their privileges are attacked they immediately go on the defensive and put up a fight; and since the world is full of complicated insecurities, since most people seem to have pet peeves of one sort or another, they are always up in arms about something.

Human society is in a permanent state of warfare about every conceivable thing. Well, says Jesus, it must not be so among you. Defer to one another. Be considerate and forgiving and unconcerned about your rights. Let God take care of them, and in the final outcome he will. One day it will be shown that it is the meek who will inherit the earth. Those who have not defended their so-called rights will be shown to have been in the right and they will enter into possession of their proper estate, while those who have guarded themselves and fought only for themselves will be shown to have made themselves poor. At the end they will have lost the most important thing of all, their own spiritual health, their souls, their real inner development as persons. Like misers, they will be found alone in some psychic attic of the spirit, counting obsessively the meaningless little victories they won, while the truly meek are out in God's own sunshine, carefree, happy inheritors of life that is life indeed. And even in this life that is true. If you are on permanent guard against the attacks of others you will cease to be able to enjoy anything, including the things you fought for. "Blessed are the meek—they shall inherit the earth."

Let me add one more word. Jesus calls us to be meek about our own rights, uncomplaining about attacks against ourselves. It does not follow that we are to be unconcerned about attacks upon others, or indifferent to their rights. The example of Jesus illuminates this fact. He was meek in the face of personal attacks, even unto death, but he was valiant in his defense of others. He battled for the oppressed and despised in all his mighty warfare against hypocrisy and self-righteousness. He mounted an assault against those who had turned God's house into a den of thieves and even robbed the poor of the consolations of worship. Christians are still called to this task. We do not defend ourselves, but we mightily defend the weak against every power that exploits them. Just think what the world would be like if those were universal human characteristics; if men and women everywhere gave up thinking about their own rights and privileges, but cared passionately for those of others. There would be marvelous economy in it all: no one's rights would ever be violated, because there would be a great balance achieved. My brother would bear my burdens and I would bear his. "Blessed are the meek—they shall inherit the earth."

*Blessed are they that hunger
and thirst after righteousness,
for they shall be filled*

If you study the Beatitudes carefully you will discover that they are interconnected: each leads on directly to the next in a great progression of truth. We have already seen the connection between those who mourn and those who are meek. There is a vital connection between those who are meek and those who hunger and thirst after righteousness. Christians, as I have said, are not to waste any precious time standing up for themselves, but they are to be passionately concerned for others' rights, they are to hunger and thirst after righteousness in the world. In each beatitude there is a subtle contrast between the way of the world and the way of Jesus. Everything is to be turned upside-down and inside-out. The worldly person battles for his own rights and cares nothing for others; by contrast, the Christian is indifferent to his own rights while he cares passionately about justice for his neighbor.

In the fourth beatitude there is another implied contrast. "Hungering and thirsting" speaks of enormous and sustained effort. We cannot do without food or drink: they are life to us. Jesus is thinking here of people whose whole life is given over to some pursuit or other; and the world is full of examples of this kind of single-mindedness. Think, for instance, of the incessant, dedicated training that an athlete puts into his quest for a gold medal. Everything else comes second: his own comfort or ease, the needs of his family, the very state of the world. Nothing matters to him except the shimmering goal that beckons: the ultimate accolade, an Olympic gold medal. That is what he hungers and thirsts for. Olympic athletes are a breed apart, but other examples could be given. Human beings are capable of the most extraordinary self-denial and heroism for the sake of anything they want badly enough. Well, says Jesus, take a leaf out of the world's book. I want you to hunger and thirst after righteousness.

This righteousness that we are to labor for has both a private and a public aspect. In the private sphere it could be translated "goodness" or "sanctity." It means that perfecting of character, that purging of all selfishness which is the mark of the saint, that spiritual thirst to be remade, to be true to the highest ideals of character. Jesus tells us that our goal is perfection, the very perfection of God. "Be ye perfect, as your heavenly Father is perfect." That is our destiny, our final destination. It is what we are made for. The only real tragedy in life is to go through it without having developed and changed and grown. The only tragedy is not to have become a saint, to have grown more like Jesus; to have wasted time on everything except the real treasure.

I often think of that memorable passage from Graham Greene's *The Power and the Glory* in which the spoiled priest sits in his condemned cell the night before his execution and sees his life laid out before him in all its pettiness and weakness and recognizes no sign of growth, no increase in sanctity. The tears roll down his cheeks at the thought of going to God empty-handed. It would, he recognizes too late, not have been impossible to have become a saint. All it needed was just a little extra bit of self-control. He felt, and the words haunt me, "as if he had missed happiness by seconds at an appointed place." If we want to be good, Jesus tells us, we can be. He will help us, if we really want it. If we really hunger and thirst after it, go after it with a will. But we don't, do we? We miss our real happiness by seconds because we are diverted to lesser goods. We hunger and thirst after things that don't last, don't satisfy, don't endure, and we go to God with nothing done at all. We miss it by seconds, those seconds in which a little act of self-denial would have taken us on stage. But we never found those few seconds that might have accumulated. We missed them, time and again, and now they have added up to a lifetime of failure.

Oh, I know that God won't reject us, brokenhearted as we are at the mess we have made of it all, but think what it might have been like if only we had hungered and thirsted after goodness, really wanted it enough to make the most of those little moments when growth would have been possible. Jesus implores us: My children, don't miss the moment at the appointed place. Give your whole heart to the quest for goodness, little by little, by a steady, slow accumulation of righteousness. "Blessed are they that hunger and thirst after righteousness, for they shall be filled." God will satisfy them.

He is waiting eagerly to respond with new strength to each little act of self-control, each little discipline of prayer, each feeble little searching after him. His children shall be filled, if they will only hunger and thirst after what he offers.

Finally, of course, we are called to work for goodness in society—each, probably, in different ways, but work we must. We are called, remember, not only to save our own souls but to be leaven in the world, salt in a corrupt society, lights in a darkened world. Christians do these things in ways small and great: they feed the hungry, even if it is only a plate of soup in a shelter for down-and-outs. They liberate captives, even if it is only by sending postcards through Amnesty International. They comfort the sorrowful, even if it is only by sitting at hospital beds and holding the hands of the anxious. In these and other ways Christians hunger and thirst after the triumph of God's righteousness. To that we are all called, for "Blessed are they that hunger and thirst after righteousness, for they shall be filled."

Blessed are the merciful,
for they shall obtain mercy

On June 5, 1968, I woke at 6:30 a.m. after a restless night in the Barth Hotel on 17th Street in Denver, Colorado. There was a radio by my bed which operated if you put in a quarter. I turned it on to hear the morning news and heard that Robert Kennedy was critically ill after an assassination attempt upon him the night before. My journal reads: "He is at this moment undergoing surgery for the removal of a bullet which is lodged in his brain." I spent the whole of that day and the following night on a train bound for San Francisco, and it wasn't until breakfast on June 6 that I heard he had died. When I got to San Francisco I went up to Grace Cathedral on Nob Hill to pray. Before the High Altar they had placed the Stars and Stripes, swathed in black and guarded by two candles, in honor of Robert Kennedy. As I prayed, I found myself crying.

I had just finished a year of study in New York, and it had ended in violence, as had most university terms that summer.

It was the year of the great student revolt. Columbia had erupted in violence, with students taking over the administration block. In Paris the students more or less took over the whole city, and in many other cities throughout the world there were pitched battles with police. It was much worse in America. Here the prevailing mood was of anger and hatred. Society was divided into groups who expressed violent contempt and hatred for each other. That mood continued for some years, both here and throughout the world, and many a university teacher has good cause to look back on those years with a shudder. The great word was polarization: people were not listening to each other. Instead, they faced each other across a great gulf and shouted slogans and obscenities at each other.

I left San Francisco that weekend in a somber mood, meditating on where it would all lead. I picked up a copy of Arthur Koestler's *Darkness at Noon,* one of the volumes of his great trilogy on the cruelty and hatred of Stalin's Russia, to read on the train. As a foreword Koestler had simply quoted a sentence from Dostoevsky: "Man, man, one cannot live quite without pity." I meditated on that sentence for hours. "Pity" has always seemed to me to be one of the loveliest words in any language, and it seemed to be the thing that was most lacking during that turbulent time. Nor is it today a characteristic of our society. It is, however, one of the characteristics that Christ praised in the Beatitudes. He said: "Blessed are the merciful, for they shall obtain mercy." The Greek word for pity or mercy is *eleos*. It is repeated every day in the Eucharist when we say *"Kyrie eleison,"* "Lord, have mercy." It is related to the Greek word *elaion,* "olive oil." Do you remember when the Good Samaritan went to the aid of the man who had fallen among thieves? Luke tells us that he poured oil into his wounds. The whole rich sense of the word "pity" or "mercy" is expressed in that act. With great gentleness and pity the Good Samaritan tended the wounds of the man fallen among thieves. He nursed him, ministered to him. From the story there comes a note of tenderness and love, of the sort that you see in a mother who cradles her small son when he has come in crying bitterly because he has fallen and bruised himself. She consoles him and bathes his knee and puts ointment on it. Her heart is filled with an enormous pity for her son. "There, there," she says, "it's all right"; and she soothes him and quiets his grief. She has pity. She shows mercy. She doesn't hector or tell him that he had no business climbing up on that wall in the first place. She doesn't scold. She has pity. She nurses him. That, says Christ, is how we ought to behave toward others. We are to be merciful. We are to recognize that all human beings, no matter how strongly we disapprove of them or disagree with them, are wounded in some real and deep sense. Even the most arrogant bully is crying inside somewhere. All human beings need to be pitied, not incessantly scolded.

Behind the biblical teaching about pity and mercy lies God's pity for us. I think that the best statement of the divine pity, this vast surge of lovingkindness that God feels for us, is found in Psalm 103:

> Like as a father pitieth his own children, even so is the Lord merciful unto them that fear him. For he knoweth whereof we are made; he remembereth that we are but dust.
>
> The Lord is full of compassion and mercy, longsuffering and of great goodness. He will not always be chiding, neither keepeth he his anger for ever.

"He will not always be chiding," unlike us much of the time with our disputes and anger and moral superiority, disapproving and arguing and organizing against each other. We forget that others are frail and vulnerable, though we are good at making excuses for our own weaknesses. What Christ wants from us is to make for others the allowances we usually make for ourselves, the allowances that God makes for all of us, remembering that we are but dust. Just think what families and nations and churches would be like if we had that attitude of tenderness and pity toward each other, if we were not always chiding. "Blessed are the merciful." Of course the beatitude does not end there: "for they shall obtain mercy." The measure you give is the measure you get. How can we plead for mercy from God if we have none for others? If we would obtain mercy we must show mercy. And even in this life we will obtain it, because people respond to kindness in others with a like warmth and kindness, while the stiff and disapproving make us stiff and unyielding in turn. "Blessed are the merciful, for they shall obtain mercy."

Blessed are the pure in heart, for they shall see God

We face an immediate difficulty when we come to the sixth beatitude, "Blessed are the pure in heart, for they shall see God." The other beatitudes give us immediately something to work on: we can learn to examine ourselves, discover the reality of our poverty; we can and probably do all mourn, from time to time at any rate; we can try to practice that attitude of meekness which opens itself in humble patience before the mystery of others. But purity of heart is far more difficult. It seems to be an original endowment of the self, and if you have not got it, it is not easy at first sight to find out how to acquire it. But what is it, anyway?

Purity of heart is often paraphrased as "singleness of purpose," and that, rather lamely, captures something of it. Again, it is probably easier to arrive at an understanding of it by studying its opposite, which is distraction, fragmentation, an inability to be satisfied with what is at hand. At its lowest and most obvious level it is captured in that old cartoon of two couples dancing cheek to cheek. The boy in one couple is gazing intently over the shoulder of his partner at the girl in the other boy's arms, and she is gazing back at him. And you feel the stirring of dissatisfaction and desire within them. Each is committed elsewhere, but they are already feeling the tug on the rope that binds them; the complications are beginning to develop. So we are talking in this beatitude about a whole range of experiences which tempt us away from the proper object of our attention, the proper focus of our devotion, to a set of other tantalizing possibilities. There is obviously a sexual implication in this beatitude. It clearly refers, in part, to that restless and undisciplined element in many natures which prevents them from really committing themselves finally and through and through to one partner, to the reality of the one-flesh relationship. They are forever tempted to get back onto the merry-go-round of sex, and consequently they never really experience the depth of a single relationship. But this does not exhaust the meaning of this beatitude.

Christ talks of a life that is aimed like an arrow which goes straight to the target; a life which gathers up its various strands, to change the analogy, and weaves them into a single cord. And we recognize this when we see it in others: that breathtaking single-mindedness which cuts through obstacles with a relaxed yet disciplined intensity. This is the hallmark of all the great souls: at some point in their lives everything is gathered together like tributaries to a great river, which then courses on with apparently effortless and unimpedable grace to the ocean which draws it. Many of the great scholars have this same quality. I remember the late Professor Ian Henderson saying to me that Karl Barth's great secret lay in the single-minded intensity he brought to his work. He told me that he spent ten hours a day at his desk, working and pondering and writing. A great mind, sweeping on and on and on. Our Lord, then, is saying something about the connection between discipline and happiness, about the interrelationship between single-minded devotion and ultimate satisfaction. And not only ultimate satisfaction, but satisfaction, too, in this present life. Though most of the beatitudes have a future reference, there is a clear implication in all of them that we can enter into the beginning of these joys even now. He is telling us that our lives must have direction, straightness, clarity; and that they must be made to go in the direction we have chosen. They must have unity, cohesion, texture; they must have the quality of whole cloth.

Alas, think of what we are! Think of the endless distractions that impede and halt and constantly redirect our progress through life. Think not only of distractions once we start, but of the postponements we make in starting at all! All those putting-off ruses we engage in, rather than take up the strangely uncongenial task. I say strangely, because we are, in fact, only postponing our joy, and we often know this as we indulge our procrastination. The secret in all this is simplicity, clarity, singleness. These are the attributes which give our lives power and vividness and joy, as they are also the marks of great art. They seem to be the purpose of God for his whole creation. But there is a strange force of inertia and complexity in the universe, dragging us away, filling our lives with unresolved complexities, fragmenting them, fraying them, dissipating them. Our society has achieved an almost demonic intensity here. Everything is churned up as by a monstrous eggbeater, scrambling and separating our dearly sought unities. Do you get the feeling of what I am trying to express? Does it ring true for you?

And here our Lord is saying, "Simplify, simplify," gather all things toward God, bring it all together. "Blessed are the pure in heart, for they shall see God"; they will be given the white stone with their name written upon it; they will be given the bright and morning star. But how? How do we begin to achieve this purity of heart? How do we make the crooked straight, the rough place plain? How do we gather together our fragmented and distracted selves into a unity?

Well, the answer is easy to give, though difficult to live by. It really boils down to a choice. We either choose purity of heart or we don't. We choose to be united and directed, or we suffer ourselves to be fragmented and distracted. There are two forces at work in the universe, the centripetal force, which seeks to draw all things into the great centrality of the Father, and the centrifugal, which seeks to blast everything out into peripheral chaos. God is constantly trying to orchestrate his universe into a harmonious unity so that he might be all in all. His is a work of continuous creation, of ordering chaos. And not out of some fascist paranoia so that the trains might run on time to the concentration camps, but so that his creation might make music together, like those "morning stars who sang together, and all the sons of God shouted for joy." And there is the force that opposes God, the god of this world, who rules by dividing and fragmenting and breaking down, whose constant aim is to disturb and destroy the ecosystem, to shatter the harmony. He it is who confounds our very language, making it prolix and opaque. (It is no accident that language is murdered in totalitarian systems of government, and tortured into Orwellian double-talk.) The lord of this world confuses and distracts our purposes, so that we are torn apart by conflicting desires. Can't you hear it, the rending, tearing, screaming noise of a universe in disintegration?

We can choose only one or the other. And we can begin only slowly, moderately, gently. This was all put with characteristic wisdom and gentleness by Baron von Hügel in one of his letters to his niece, Gwen:

> If we want our fervour to last, we must practice moderation even in our prayer, even in our Quiet. And certainly it is perseverance in the spiritual life, on and on, across the years and the changes of our moods and trials, health and environment: it is this that supremely matters. And you will, Gwen, add greatly to the probabilities of such perseverance, if you will get into the way of keeping a little even beyond this (set) time (of prayer), when you are dry, and a little short of this time when you are in consolation. You see why, don't you?—Already the Stoics had the grand double rule: abstine et sustine, 'abstain and sustain', i.e. moderate thyself in things attractive and consoling, persevere, hold out, in things repulsive and desolating. There is nothing God loves better, or rewards more richly, than such double self-conquest as this! (*Letters to a Niece*; London: Dent, 1950, p. 67).

We either choose purity, singleness of heart, and the vision of God, the knowledge of the oneness, the unity of all that is: or we choose to shatter the glass into fragments, to knock Humpty Dumpty off his wall, with little chance of putting him back together again.

Ask yourself where your life is going, what you are doing with it. See whether it is characterized by unity or division, and pledge yourself anew to purity of heart, to the quest for that vision you were born longing to see and can too easily forfeit. For this is true happiness and true blessedness, to see God.

> O Father, give the Spirit power to climb
> To the foundation of all light, and be purified.
> Break through the mists of earth, the weight of the
>   clod,
> Shine forth in splendour, Thou that art calm weather,
> And quiet resting place for faithful souls.
> To see thee is the end and the beginning,

Thou carriest us, and thou dost go before,
Thou art the journey, and the journey's end.

                                        Boethius

Blessed are the peacemakers,
for they shall be called sons of God

The seventh beatitude is, in many ways, the most difficult to
talk about with any directness. The other beatitudes refer to
attitudes that have a mainly private reference: they are terribly
difficult to follow, but at least the application is reasonably
plain. The case is very different with this beatitude about making peace: at one level the agonizing and painful question is
not *whether* one should make peace, but *how* one should do it.

To begin with, the matter is reasonably simple. Christians
are called to be not just passive and nonaggressive, but active
in making peace, in reconciling enemies, in breaking down
fences and barriers between people. They are to be peacemakers, following the example of God himself, who, according to
Paul, made peace with us through the cross of Christ. When
God reconciled the world to himself he took the initiative, he
acted first. As John puts it in his first letter: We love because
God loved us first. The conclusion is obvious, isn't it? Those
who would follow Christ take peacemaking, reconciling initiatives: they do not wait for the other person to come around,
they take the first step. At one level, the applications are
straightforward. In our personal relations we can try to live by
this beatitude: the family is the best place to start. Never let the
sun go down on your wrath. Never nurse a sullen resentment
into one of those exquisitely long silences by which you punish
others for daring to disagree with you or criticize you: those
hurt looks, that tight little face all drawn in in pained incomprehension. Christians are not to enjoy the luxury of this kind
of emotional warfare. They are peacemakers: they get over
their resentments quickly, they laugh off the cutting remark,
they take the first step toward the other. And the same approach is to apply in all our group relations: in the church, at
our place of work. We are actively to make peace where it has
broken down, and not only with those who oppose us: we are

to be reconcilers of others, though we must remember that this usually calls for enormous tact and sensitivity. This beatitude is fundamental, and you can see why. In our group relations as well as in our personal relationships we are prone to all sorts of misunderstandings, we are liable to find ourselves in situations of complex hostility, because all of us are in some sense selfish and immature and wounded. Few among us are peacemakers, but many are adept at stirring up trouble, and many love to stand by and watch the spectacle of a good quarrel, helping the poison to circulate by our very eagerness to hear every obsessive little detail. There is, you see, something sick and distorted about human nature, so these conflicts are inevitable, they are part of the very structure of human relationships. God's great desire is to heal this disease, to purify the poisoned well: so he acts, he gives himself in Christ, he *makes* peace. And he longs for us to join him in this godlike task; that is why peacemakers are called "sons of God."

Now, all of that is very difficult to follow, but it is not too difficult to understand. Settling a quarrel between two members of a family is often taxing and tedious, but it is usually manageable, given patience. But when you move into more and more complex group arrangements, it becomes correspondingly more difficult to apply the peacemaking principle. Think how complex and fraught are the relationships between, say, trade unions and employers, or between the different social classes in our class-ridden society. Think of the extraordinary tangle of factors in any single industrial dispute, yet think of our constant weakness for simplifying it to a straightforward conflict between good guys and bad guys. Now move up the scale: think of the enormously complicated background of sectarian bitterness in a place like Northern Ireland. Move further up the scale: think of the intricacy of all the factors involved in the tension between the USSR and the Western Alliance— a complex of historical, racial, psychological, ideological, and economic elements all densely packed together into a great lump of fear and distrust. The question very soon becomes not, why don't we make peace? but how on earth are we to make peace, where can we start, what is the quarrel really about, who speaks for whom, at what level do we start the peacemaking process?

Only the naive imagine that peacemaking at this level is straightforward. There are occasions, of course, when a single act of magnanimity pushes things forward, such as Mr. Sadat's decision to go to Israel. But think how soon that peacemaking gesture was swallowed up by the interminable negotiations that followed. It is important to recognize a number of factors here, if you are to avoid the traditional Christian disease of reducing complex situations to simple slogans. The first is very difficult for a certain kind of Christian to accept, but it seems to be inescapable: the larger a group becomes, the less susceptible it is to simple moral pressure.

At the level of the nation-state this rule becomes absolute, and can be formulated into the truism that the foreign policy of any nation is always and only motivated by self-interest. According to certain moral theologians there is no point in trying to apply to states moral principles that might influence individuals: they are totally different creatures. States use the rhetoric of moral behavior, but in fact they always follow their own interests exclusively. Reinhold Niebuhr, perhaps *the* social philosopher of our century, turned it all into a simple epigram: Moral Man and Immoral Society, which was the title of one of his most influential books. His great message to the church was that it ought to recognize how different these two realities are, and not try to apply private morality to collective realities. If this distinction is true, if all governments operate on the basis of national self-interest and are unable to operate on any other *by definition,* then how do Christians apply the peacemaking imperative to the nations they belong to? (Incidentally, we get no help from Jesus here: he offered absolutely no advice on conducting the affairs of nations; all his challenges were made at the individual level.) Now, you may not accept the self-interest theory of nation-states (though you will find it difficult to come up with examples of any state that does not put its at the individual level.)

Now, you may not accept the self-interest theory of nation-states (though you will find it difficult to come up with examples of any state that does not put its own interests first). You may believe that it is possible to educate nations and governments, to improve them, refine them. Undoubtedly there is something in that, though I have a sneaking suspicion that it is applicable in only a few countries. In most of them the government does not take kindly to such moral exhortations. Even so, let us allow the basic claim, that governments can and ought to be morally influenced by their citizens. We come up against the fact that group relations on the international scale pose enormous difficulties for the moralist, because nations, as such, are not simple moral agents with a single nervous system and set of ideas. The larger and more complicated the group becomes, the less susceptible it is to any kind of moral challenge. We understand something of this phenomenon, but much of it is mysterious to us: why do people find it easy to behave badly in groups in ways they would never dream of in more private relationships? Think of the chanting, hate-filled mobs we have seen on our TV screens: privately, they are probably all very nice people, no worse than you or I, but get them in a mob and something happens. Psychologists talk about the herd instinct or mob psychology, but these are only descriptive terms; they do not help us to understand why it happens. The fact is, it does. The larger the group, the less personal, the less moral, the less compassionate or persuadable it is. When you get to almost abstract entities like nations, you have moved almost completely into a set of relations that are hardly governed by moral factors at all. This accounts for the frustrations many private individuals of strong moral conviction feel as they confront mankind in its collective aspect. They do not seem to be speaking the same language. In fact, most of the time they are not.

Now, all of this makes it incredibly difficult for Christians to apply the beatitude about peacemaking to international or intergroup affairs. This difficulty has led to several responses down the centuries from Christians who have wrestled with the problem. One of the most attractive responses is to cut off all ties with the rest of society: states and nations and societies are evil, they are immoral in their relations with each other; there is no way you can be involved in their affairs without being corrupted, therefore Christians must simply step aside from the world which is perishing and create the perfect society within the Christian family. That is where you can live the perfect life. In society you cannot. So you leave society: you do not vote, you will not join the armed forces even if your country is invaded, you may even refuse to pay taxes, since they are the very basis on which the power of the state is built.

That is normally thought of as the sectarian response: few Christian groups follow it today, though there are many examples of groups who have.

A more common approach to the problem is for the Christian to work within the political traditions which are found in the world. Indeed, there is a lot of evidence which shows that the thinking of Christians has itself deeply influenced and formed the world's political institutions. But here Christians are faced with a real theological dilemma. The most dramatic political debate in history is that between reformers and revolutionaries, and Christians find themselves on different sides in the conflict. Though the debate appears to be between political revolutionaries and reformers, it is really based on an age-old theological dilemma about the nature of man and his institutions.

Western political structures are based on a doctrine of original sin. From St. Paul to Sir Karl Popper, many influential Western thinkers have viewed man and his ideals with affectionate scepticism. A study of history provides the student with adequate empirical verification for the doctrine of original sin. Man's nature is tainted with a radical egotism which vitiates his best purposes and corrupts his noblest institutions. It is seen at its most chronic when man assumes power over his fellows. It is not power which corrupts man. It is man's original corruption which leads to the inevitable misuse of power. Any political philosophy which recognizes this profound fact will have two major characteristics.

First, it will possess a fundamental mistrust of those who wield power. This, in turn, will lead to a system which disperses power as widely as possible in order to balance and counteract abuses. The final form of power-dispersion is found in democracy, an untidy method of government which has not yet been improved upon. The essential need for democracy is summed up in Reinhold Niebuhr's famous epigram:

> Man's capacity for justice makes democracy possible;
> but man's inclination to injustice makes democracy
>   necessary.

Secondly, there will be a mistrust of all visionary programs for social change. But this pessimistic assessment of man's utopian projects will not necessarily lead to political quietism. On the contrary, man will tackle the much more realistic task of eliminating identifiable injustices. Popper calls this "protectionism," the technique of protecting the weak against the frequently sinful energies of the strong, while allowing a proper measure of freedom for man's creative initiatives.

These are the main characteristics of the reformist political systems of the West and their various versions of welfare capitalism. It is an intriguing paradox that a method which is based on such a pessimistic anthropology has so greatly increased the freedom and welfare of millions during the last century.

In marked contrast to this approach, the emergent political philosophies of the Third World are utopian and are based on an often unconsciously held doctrine of original righteousness. Central to this outlook is the conviction that man can create a just and perfect society if he gets the program right. On this view, the hideous injustices which characterize man's history are the result, not of incurable sinfulness in man's nature, but of a structural flaw in the institutions he has created. Since he is capable of achieving the Good Life, the obstacles which seem to be permanently placed in the way of that achievement must be caused by the intervention of hostile agents: "An enemy hath done this." The utopian outlook, therefore, develops what Popper calls "the conspiracy theory" of evil. Our century has been particularly rich in conspiracy theories both of the Right and the Left. A political philosophy which is based on this approach will have two marked characteristics.

First, it leads to a centralization of power: the good have the right and the duty to rule; and this concentration of power is necessary if the enemies of the vision are to be adequately dealt with. Secondly, it leads to a strongly directed political program aimed at bringing specifically good things to pass. It is not interested in moderating the effect of evil institutions. It refuses to "tinker with the System." Instead, it is passionately intent upon rebuilding a New Society from top to bottom.

Utopians are usually fired by a strong passion for freedom and justice. It is an intriguing paradox, therefore, that their pursuit of justice leads almost invariably to a serious diminishment of freedom.

The anguish which many of us in the West feel as we watch the revolutionary turmoil of the Third World is that, while we share their anger and outrage at the misery and oppression which afflicts the vast majority of the world's population, our own experience and our reading of history have bred in us a profound mistrust of revolutionary programs of social change. On the other hand, the great weakness of the kind of political realism we have developed is that it provides no short-term hope for the oppressed. It is essentially gradualist in its methods and convictions. It lacks eschatological flair.

In this it is in strong contrast to Marxism, which is essentially a political eschatology. This accounts for the amazing survival of Marxism in spite of a hundred years of relentless falsification both of Marxist prediction and of Marxist planning. Marxism survives because it claims to be the Politics of Hope. Our challenge as we face our revolutionary brethren from the Third World is the problem of finding a political hope for the present that will not mortgage the future to a more terrible bondage.

Let me try to sum up. Christians are called to be peacemakers. Peacemaking is painful enough in the personal sphere, because you have to take the first step and initiate the reconciliation, if you are a Christian. However, this peacemaking role becomes more difficult to apply as you move up the scale of human community. A different set of dynamics operates between large groups than between individuals, so it is particularly hard to find the appropriate way to make peace. The complications increase: it goes without saying that Christians are in favor of peace and against war, against poverty and injustice and oppression. These are ends which all Christians share. The vexing thing is that Christians down the centuries have differed very radically in the means they have espoused to achieve these ends, and continue so to differ. Unfortunately, there is no obvious word of Jesus' that we can appeal to that might arbitrate the quarrel which has gone on among Christian thinkers for two thousand years on this subject. Jesus seems determined to leave certain matters to us: he has provided us with principles; now, he says, go out into the complexities of my world and wrestle with the difficulties, as you hold my principles in your mind.

Blessed are those who are persecuted for righteousness' sake, for theirs is the kingdom of heaven. Blessed are you when men revile you and persecute you and utter all kinds of evil against you falsely on my account. Rejoice and be glad, for your reward is great in heaven, for so men persecuted the prophets who were before you.

The Beatitudes give us a marvelously comprehensive account of the life of Christian goodness. They are comprehensive, inclusive, in two ways. First of all in the total range of conduct which they cover. Secondly because they are just as concerned with personal goodness as with social witness. They show us that Christian morality is both public and private, and that we cannot take our pick: Christian goodness is inclusive in its scope, it covers every aspect of life. Let me rehearse again the main significance of each beatitude.

"The poor in spirit." This has a double meaning. The happy person is detached from this world's goods. He knows that here there is no abiding city, so he does not invest too much of himself in material possessions, in reputation or status. But the person who is poor in spirit also knows his own need for God, his spiritual poverty and inadequacy. He is not sufficient to himself alone. The New English Bible translates this beatitude "Blessed are those who know their need for God."

"Those who mourn." The Christian mourns over the sorrow and pain of the world. He is not indifferent to human need. He is a mourner, a person of dynamic compassion. But there is a private dimension as well. The person who mourns knows himself to be a sinner, in need of forgiveness and the endless grace of God's mercy, so he mourns his own sinfulness. He is not complacent about himself. He mourns.

"Blessed are the meek." The meek person is not a moral bully. He knows his own lack of goodness and worth, so he is not tempted to throw his spiritual weight around. He is the opposite of the preacher described by Reinhold Niebuhr:

Think of sitting Sunday after Sunday under some professional holy man who is constantly asserting his egotism by criticizing yours. A spiritual leader who has too many illusions is useless. One who has lost his illusions about mankind and retains his illusions about himself is insufferable. Let the process of disillusionment continue until the self is included *(Leaves from the Notebooks of a Tamed Cynic*; New York: Living Age Books, 1960, p. 112).

Well, the meek person has lost all his illusions about himself. He does not go around parading his righteousness by accusing others of unrighteousness.

"Those who hunger and thirst after righteousness." Again, there is a private and a public side to this beatitude. The Christian seeking to follow the pattern of Christ is called to hunger and thirst after personal goodness and holiness. He is to seek it as though his life depended upon it. But personal goodness or righteousness is not enough. He has to struggle for a kinder and more just society. He is to be mindful of the poor. He is to champion the oppressed.

"The merciful." The Christian is not to be strident and harsh in his attitude to others, even if he disapproves of them or disagrees with them. He is not to chide. He is to be merciful, full of pity, as he remembers his own need of mercy and God's mercy toward him.

"The pure in heart, the single-minded." This beatitude contains chastity and fidelity, but it is wider in its scope. The person who is pure in heart brings his life together under the mighty purpose of holiness. He is not a devious person, a fixer, a complicated schemer, but a simple, straightforward person whose life has clarity and directness and who brings these characteristics into his dealings with others. This beatitude presupposes discipline and order in life. The person who is pure in heart is the opposite of the person whose life is fragmented and disordered. Happy are the single-minded.

"The peacemakers." Here, again, the two aspects are important. Christians are to be reconcilers in their private relations and in their work for peace and stability on earth. There is to be no division. There is no point in being a private reconciler if you do not also have a care for the wider aspects of peacemaking amid the complicated violence in the world. On the other hand, there is great dishonesty in being a professional peaceworker in the political sphere if you are a quarrelsome and contentious person at home or in your local congregation.

In other words, there must be a struggle in our lives toward integrity between the personal and the public dimensions of goodness. There is an old Edinburgh proverb about the man who was an angel on the causeway but a devil at home. It is this comprehensiveness that imposes the greatest strain on the Christian. We are all tempted to be selective in our pursuit of the holiness of Christ: some are attracted to the field of public and prophetic goodness in society, but lead private lives of great personal disorder. Others lead lives of great personal rectitude but have no care for those outside their own immediate circle. Christ calls us to follow him closely in both aspects of life.

And it is this that brings us to the last and most unusual of the Beatitudes.

Blessed are those who are persecuted for righteousness' sake, for theirs is the kingdom of heaven. Blessed are you when men revile you and persecute you and utter all kinds of evil against you falsely on my account. Rejoice and be glad, for your reward is great in heaven, for so men persecuted the prophets who were before you.

In this final beatitude Christ takes it for granted that if you seek to follow this way of holiness you will be reviled and persecuted. This is a matter of straight historical record. Whenever Christians have tried to live out the Beatitudes they have come up against the ugly side of the world, without exception. They are either reviled or persecuted, or both. But there is a subtle twist to this beatitude and its outworking in history. I said that most Christians are selective in their following of Christ. This is often an unconscious process. They follow those parts of the Christian way of life that happen to be socially acceptable in the place and time where they live, while managing to avoid the more controversial and dangerous parts. And we all do it, so be aware of what is happening. Let me give you some examples from other places and other times, before

zeroing in on the situation here today. In Russia today, it is
perfectly acceptable to the authorities for Christians to follow
the way of private holiness. Christians will not get into trouble
if, as the sociologists put it, they "privatize" their religion, keep
it in the private sphere. Once they go public and prophetic it
is a different story. For instance, if a congregation decided to
mount a campaign for the freeing of political prisoners or
against Soviet anti-Semitism or against the Russian invasion of
Afghanistan, it would have the KGB down upon it in a moment. I am not judging them. I would be just as selective. The
fact remains that they have to be selective if they would avoid
persecution.

The same is true in South Africa. The government there
has no objection to piety and personal religion, but once
churchmen go public and seek to follow the Beatitudes into
the political sphere, they are in trouble, as many of them are
at this moment.

Let us go back a hundred years to Victorian Britain. There
was great emphasis then upon private Christian morality, and
Victorian Christians, by and large, were privately more moral
in their personal relations, in their respect for the sanctity of
marriage, in their commitment to telling the truth, than is our
society. But they showed a marked disinclination to question
the public injustices of their society, the glaring inequalities that
existed, the sweating of the poor, the employment of children
in factories and coal mines. Speaking out on those issues brought
ridicule and derision and social ostracism.

Wherever you go in time and place you find that the
Christian witness to the total holiness of Christ is selective. You
would expect, therefore, to find the same thing in our day, and
you would be right. There are moral fashions today, as there
were a hundred years ago. There are fashionable causes which
no one will trouble you for embracing, though there may not
be much room left on the bandwagon. But there are large
areas in our moral life which it is unfashionable to espouse,
and to do so can lead to ridicule and derision. I said that the
Beatitudes have a personal and a public aspect. In our society
it is the public aspect which is fashionable. (Just because it is
fashionable, of course, does not make it invalid, though it may
make it easier to espouse.) Today there is a great emphasis on

what used to be called "the social gospel." This is a perfectly proper side of the total Christian commitment, a side which was almost completely lacking in Victorian days. Today we are used to Christians' taking a strong stand on unemployment, on racism and sexism, on the economic injustices of the world. Christians argue about their approaches to these controversial topics, but they are at least out in the open. What I think is being ignored in the West today is the private side of the total Christian life-style. The prevailing moral attitude in the West today has been described by Harry Blamires as "middle-class Hedonism." The pursuit of pleasure, either through conspicuous consumption, or through a swinging, value-free sexual adventurism, is the norm in our society. There is considerable evidence, too, that this prevailing attitude has infiltrated the church. Campaigners for sexual chastity, opponents of pornography, people who object to the violence and nihilism of many films and television programs, are openly derided and ridiculed by the opinion-formers in our society. What, for instance, is your attitude to the Moral Majority in America or the Festival of Light in Britain? The chances are that many of you will react to them with a snort of fashionable contempt. Is it not possible that your reaction owes more to the influence of the newspapers you read than to the New Testament? We look back on the Victorians with incredulity. We say, "How could they just ignore the state of their society, be apparently unaware of the appalling injustices of their day, or even be actively involved in their perpetuation?" And we are scandalized. Is it not possible that in the 21st century Christians will look back on the sexual disarray of the West today, with its fashionable pursuit of the *Playboy* theory of sex, and wonder that the church was so taken in by it, so that it lost the will to preach about personal morality? Will they conclude that we were afraid of the fashionable derision of the opinion-formers of our society? Will they say that we sold out to the spirit of the age because we were afraid of that subtle persecution from our contemporaries who could reduce us to panic by daring to suggest that we might be conservative and old-fashioned?

It is very difficult to follow Christ with our whole heart and soul and mind. Most of us shrink from unpopularity and persecution. Today we will not be sent to a concentration camp for preaching the gospel publicly, but there are subtle ways of persecution which are even more effective than a policeman's rifle butt. Few of us like to be derided, or thought reactionary or behind-the-times. That, for us, is the contemporary mode of persecution, and it becomes increasingly prevalent as the moral values of our society become increasingly hedonistic in private matters. Christ wants us to continue to embrace the social implications of his way, but he does not want us to neglect the sphere of personal morality, even though we are laughed at. One final word. The voices that perplex and weaken us may not come from outside all the time, either. We are formed by the moral fashions of the day. Our standards can be eroded by the prevailing culture. In South Africa it is difficult for a white Christian to avoid a subtle and gradual change in his attitude toward racism, till one day he finds himself agreeing with the prevailing heresy of the ruling group. The sàme thing happens to us. Society molds us after its own image. If we refuse to be molded, it turns on us with ridicule or persecution. We are all, therefore, tempted to selective obedience, and we never notice it is happening, though we can see it in others. By his Beatitudes Christ calls us to a life of tension and struggle as we seek to follow him with our whole life. We are not to pick and choose, even though it leads to suffering. We have his promise, after all:

> Blessed are you when men revile you and persecute you and utter all kinds of evil against you falsely on my account. Rejoice and be glad, for your reward is great in heaven, for so men persecuted the prophets who were before you.

Epilogue

CHAPTER TEN

The Faith of a Hypocrite

I have called this chapter "The Faith of a Hypocrite" because I am a hypocrite. The original Greek meaning of the word was precise: it meant an actor, someone who, in Greek drama, hid his face behind a mask and played a part on the stage. The evolution of the word after that will be obvious, but Jesus gave it a rather new twist. He condemned those who performed their religious observance "to be seen of men"; but one feels that this type of hypocrisy is more amusing than deadly. He tells us that such men "have their reward." They are applauded by their fellows and receive a reputation for piety. Much more serious was the kind of hypocrisy which totally misunderstood the real nature of religion. This kind of hypocrite is not merely pretending to be what he is not. He is, in fact, in the grip of a lie. He has replaced real devotion to God with a religious system which he follows with idolatrous exactness. His real danger is not that he is a rather amusing spiritual buffoon who makes religion an object of contempt, but that he seriously misleads people as to the real nature of God. He is "a blind guide" who places obstacles in the way of those who are struggling toward God. This is a permanent criticism of all institutional religion and its representatives. There is a permanent pathological dynamic in religious systems which tends toward this kind of idolatry. A study of the history of Christianity provides many examples of this process at work, and it is still a danger. We elevate our systems into enormous hurdles which prevent men and women from finding the God whom they seek. And in all these ways I am, and have been, a hypocrite.

But here I am using the word in yet another, possibly very
modern sense. My difficulty is not that I am pretending to be
what I am not, but that I find it difficult to be what I am, a
Christian.

But it is even more complicated than that! It is not simply
that I know what, as a Christian, I ought to do but cannot do
it. That dilemma is a permanent inheritance of the Christian,
and no one has put it better than Paul:

> I do not understand my own actions. For I do not do
> what I want, but I do the very thing I hate. . . . I can will
> what is right, but I cannot do it. For I do not do the good
> I want, but the evil I do not want is what I do (Romans
> 8:15ff.).

What Paul described for all time is the problem of moral
impotence, of finding no correspondence between knowledge
of what is good and the power to do it. That is bad enough.
What is almost as bad is the dilemma of the Christian who
wants to do what is right and good but who is not sure what
it is. And that is the position many Christians find themselves
in today: it is not just a problem of will, it is a problem of
knowledge. We are beset on all sides with extraordinary moral
and theological difficulties, and it is not at all easy to say without
fear of contradiction what the Christian solution is. Of course,
not all Christians are in this predicament. Some have an enviable certainty as to the precise Christian response to most of
these dilemmas. I have no desire to mock those who possess
such certainty. Each of us must follow his own conscience, and
I strongly approve of those who know what is right and seek
to do it, come hell or high water. I would, however, like to
register a minor protest. For a lot of us today, many of the
issues that face us are not patient of a simple solution. It would
be easier for us if they were. But our hesitations and ambi-
guities are not necessarily evidence of moral or theological flab-
biness: they could be evidence of respect for the complex ways
in which truth is discovered and decisions are made.

I said I was a hypocrite, not because I pretended to be
what I was not, but because I find it difficult to be what I am,
a Christian. And I went on to say something about situations

of moral doubt. But my hypocrisy is much deeper than that. Mark Twain said that it wasn't the parts of the Bible he didn't understand that bothered him; it was the parts he did understand. Anyone who has grown at all in the knowledge of God as made known by Jesus Christ feels an awful demand laid upon him. Jesus Christ is not simply the object of our faith, the One we believe in. He is the exemplar of our faith, he is the Way we ought to believe. In him we see the proper and perfect response to God: total and utterly unself-regarding trust. The example of Jesus fills me with longing and with dread: longing, because the logic and instinct of faith is to trust the Father utterly; dread, because I know I cannot do it. And here my predicament is not theoretical, it is not because I do not know what I ought to do. Like Mark Twain, I know only too well. In all sorts of situations a quite specific demand is laid upon me, and I refuse it. The core of that demand is found in the Sermon on the Mount. It turns my values and standards upside down. It is a complete transvaluation of all human values, a reversal of all human standards. By all standards, it is a piece of sublime and heart-rending insanity. "Happy are the hungry, the hated, the persecuted." Happy! Blessed! "And woe to the rich, the satisfied, the successful, the happy." Woe to my whole way of life, which is a modest striving for more security and wealth and success. The Sermon goes on to pile paradox on scandal, and scandal on paradox.

> Love your enemies. Do not resist evil. Turn the other cheek when you are assaulted. When you are robbed, run after the thief and tell him he forgot the family silver, and would he like to borrow your car to make an easier getaway?

The wild logic of Christ seems simple: take any natural impulse, any commonsense reaction, any proper institutional or personal prudence, reverse it utterly, and go and do it! And at the root of it all, beneath all the scandalous exaggeration, lies a radical trust in God which is to come before everything else, no matter where it leads us. And I cannot argue that it is an eschatological poem, unrealizable in this world of imperious necessities, because I have seen it realized and heard of it in other times and places. It was the way of Christ himself, and it is a way which is followed by a few flaming souls in every generation. And I know it is the only answer to the torment and anguish of the world. I know that those who live thus, somehow redeem the rest of us. I am a Christian. I love Christ, but I cannot follow him. I refuse the absolute demand, but I allow him a moderate influence upon me. I will not give away all my goods to feed the poor, but I try to be moderately charitable to a few good causes. I cannot love my enemies, but, when I remember, I try to curb my temper. I turn the blazing and reckless love of Christ into a benign and not too upsetting and satisfactorily generalized goodwill. I form the image of the poor and angry man of Nazareth into that of a mild and well-intended middle-class clergyman! This is my deepest hypocrisy, and I intend to continue it. Why? Why do I continue to call myself a Christian when I quite clearly and self-consciously refuse to accept the absolute demand of the gospel of Jesus Christ?

My answer to that, and the only thing that keeps me a Christian, is the certainty that the gospel is not primarily a demand but a gift, and that only when the gift is fully received and fully understood does the demand become possible. It seems to me that the Christian church has too often reversed that process. She has insisted upon the demand, or upon her current version of it, without mediating the grace that makes it possible. It is this reversal which makes much of the church's moral rhetoric futile. But what is the gift? and where do we see it given? We see it in the suffering and death of Christ. By an audacious strategy of the divine love, the Father takes the demand which is laid upon us and fulfils it through the sacrifice of his Son.

The sublime and staggering claim which is made in the New Testament is that God, "who was in Christ," was in some sense himself our victim, and that he was acting in that horrifying execution on our behalf. How can language contain that extraordinary claim? The burden of his message and of his life shows that, for Jesus, our sin was not an ultimate obstacle to our relationship with God. Or rather, that *conscious* sin was not an obstacle while unconscious sin apparently was! This is clearly contrary to both traditional and modern moral theology, which holds that unconscious sin is not, by definition, sin at all, since it is not a conscious act. Of course, "unconscious sin" can be morally culpable if there is evidence that the sinner should have informed his conscience, and that he bears a responsibility for his own blindness. But that, anyway, is not the point I am making here. Jesus used his anger and his fiercest condemnations for those who did not know they were sinners, while those who were acknowledged as such, and so acknowledged themselves, were given every assurance of love and forgiveness. The point seems to be that sin, as such, does not keep us from God, but only that exceeding sinful sin which does not know the reality of its own condition. The real offense in this sin which is blind to its own condition is that it does not acknowledge the desperate impotence of man, the utter lostness that sees God afar off and does not so much as lift up its head. When *that* condition is acknowledged, we recognize with the publicans and sinners that what we *cannot* achieve is given to us. God lays a demand upon us which we are unable to fulfil, but he sends forth his own Son to fulfil it on our behalf, and makes his obedience a gift to us. And it is desperately important, both for Jesus and for Paul, that we realize our true estate as beggars who have been brought into the feast, and not start behaving like the palace major domo. In other words, we are, by definition, sinners, always sinners, who live by the gracious gift of God. No matter the degree of intimacy to which the Father calls us, even in that state which Paul calls adopted sonship, we hold it not by right or by might but only by grace. We are always justified *sinners*, sanctified sinners, so we have no right to throw our moral weight about.

However, the whole religious tendency of mankind and of Christianity is to reverse all this and treat our relationship with God as a graduated examination system in which we work our way up to God. Or we see God as the guardian of the moral code, keeping careful watch over the celestial computer which tabulates our every act and tots up our score. All these images or similes for our relationship with God are essentially formal, authoritarian, and objective. We are always being measured against standards. It is this way of understanding our relationship with God which Jesus came to undermine. God's attitude toward us is governed only by the passionate subjectivity of love. His very anger at our sin is another aspect of a love that fears we are damaging ourselves. On the night before he suffered, according to St. John, Jesus washed the feet of his disciples; he performed the most menial of all household tasks, the work of the houseboy. That, too, is the action of God. He washes our feet. He is our servant as well as our victim. He rescues us, ransoms us from the bondage of our anxious self-ishness, not by an act of power and overwhelming justice, but by an act of self-emptying love. He woos us, this God of ours, he defeats us by the lengths to which he'll go. He allows us to push him right out of the world onto a cross. And this is where the picture becomes painfully familiar. I hear the great demand of God in the Sermon on the Mount and I reject it, but now I see it, not as a demand *I* can fulfil, but as the story of God's way with me. We are his enemies, yet he endlessly blesses us, stretching out his hands toward us every day, the eternal beggar; we are the thieves who pillage and destroy what is his, and he says to us, "My children, here is more and more"; and we are they who would attack him, so he opens his hands upon all our crosses and stretches out his feet to the nails we drive in day after day. It is *his* way with *us* which is depicted in the great demand. It is the demand he makes upon himself till the end of time. It is his way with us until we give up the hopeless struggle against that overwhelming and utterly unshamable love and go to him, defeated at last, not by his power but by his unconquerable weakness. This is the foundation stone of the Christian message, and this is why we call that message "gospel" or "good news."

Of course, many things follow from this astonishing piece of news, including that whole response we call holiness; but it is important to get the order right. Holiness is the response of love and gratitude to the amazing gift of God in Christ; it is not a set of behavioral responses imposed upon us by a superior power. The vision of the holiness of God calls forth in our hearts a response that is both longing, longing to be like that, to be as he is; and self-condemnation, because we know we are not like that at all and have no power within ourselves to be like that. And it is here that the psychological wisdom of God becomes clear, if I can speak like that. The condition we call Original Sin seems to have as one of its central ingredients a fear and hatred of God. Yet we long for him in the core of our being and are drawn toward him, toward the Other who completes and fills up our lack. So, like everything else about us, this longing is distorted and mangled by our self-will and almost unconscious fear of finding him. Our blinded longing plunges about in many directions, seeking that we might not find, or seeking with a studious absent-mindedness, because we are not sure how he will receive us. And all the longing for God is forced in other directions. Almost everything that we call sin is, in fact, a blinded and disorganized and perverted search for him who is our peace. God's strategy of redemption, therefore, seems aimed at removing our fears, at waking in us a real nostalgia for himself by showing us his real nature of everlasting love. He *woos* us into holiness. In the strange words of St. Augustine, God grants to us what he demands of us. But our insecurity is so deeply rooted that we never fully accept the gospel, so we are never fully able to offer ourselves wholeheartedly. So the Christian life becomes a nursing program, in which we are gently and gradually, with many remissions, drawn back toward health. And in that great sanitarium we call the Church, the patients are all at different stages of growth toward health, but none is fully cured. And, alas, there is a strange tendency in those who are, perhaps, a little stronger than others to forget the nature of their own infirmity. Gradually, the order of the gospel is reversed by the institution that claims to enshrine it, and we end, not with acceptance leading to holiness, but with holiness as the price we pay for acceptance. Perhaps the most gruesome reversal of all is that we end by demanding health as a qualification for entrance into the sanitarium which was established for the sick. And the representatives of the one who came to call the sick end by demanding a clean bill of health from those who would partake of the medicine of salvation.

I can already hear the obvious protest:

the Christian Church is not a nursing home, it is an army on the march and its members are called to an arduous life of struggle and commitment. It is called to challenge and oppose the tyranny of sin, not feebly compromise with it.

Well, that is undoubtedly an authentic biblical note. It is the note of prophecy. It is the note that Christ struck when he summoned his disciples to take up the cross and follow him. It is the voice of the wrath of God "revealed from heaven against all ungodliness and wickedness of men." It is a word from God we must hear, but is it God's last word? In my weakness and hypocrisy I believe it is not. His last word was the word of his own dying for us, stamped and ratified by the sign of his rising. God has again relented. His love has triumphed over his justice, his tenderness has overcome his anger. Every pastor knows something of this dilemma. He knows his own weakness, but he also knows those to whom he is sent with the word of God. He knows there are few soldiers of Christ, though there are many who are wounded and lost. Christ's army exists, but it resembles a field hospital more than a regiment on the march. The paradox is resolved for us by the mystery of the rising of Christ. In some strange sense the victory is already accomplished, though we continue to labor through the battle. We are told that we are already saved, though we do not often see in our lives the signs of the holiness that has been won for us. The last word from God is, after all, the word of grace. He has visited and redeemed us. What remains is to try to live up to the gift we have been given. Let me end by quoting some amazing words:

> Christian art is joyous because it is free, and it is free because of the fact of Christ's having died to redeem the world. One need not die in art nor save the world in it, those matters having been, so to speak, attended to. What is left? The blissful responsibility to enjoy the world (Nadezhda Mandelstam, *Hope Against Hope*; London: Collins, 1971, p. x).

And these are not cheap words. They come from Osip Mandelstam, the greatest Russian poet of this century, who was hounded to death by Stalin in 1938. Christ has been raised from the dead. What is left? The blissful responsibility to enjoy the world.